THE CREDIT GAME

ENTREPRENEUR SECRETS TO BUILDING BUSINESS CREDIT WITHOUT PERSONAL LIABILITY USING EIN

CHEVON K. PATRICK

ISBN: 979-8-9865784-2-2

FREE GIFT FOR READERS

JUST FOR YOU!

Or Visit: https://www.bit.ly/TCGgift

INTRODUCTION

"Money is a terrible master but an excellent servant."
— P. T. Barnum

Too many people today believe they can't start a business because they don't have the startup capital. After all, you've got to spend money to make money, right? Renting space, buying equipment, hiring employees, and paying for marketing costs are not things the average citizen thinks they can afford.

I'm here to show you how anyone can start a business with no initial credit checks that result in hard inquiries, no cash flow, and no collateral. These are all qualifying factors that traditional lenders require, and they are the factors that limit most business startups' success. This alternative method of funding will not only help you obtain the capital you need, but will also give you time to improve your personal credit if needed. My previous book, *The Credit Game: Plays We Were Never Taught*, can help you with that as well.

The secret here is that most people who successfully start businesses, no matter how wealthy they are or aren't, don't spend their own money to do it. Instead, they use business credit.

My goal with this book is to empower you to start a business that thrives. If you don't think you have the wealth or skills to start a successful business, we'll change that here. And if you already own a business, but it's struggling financially, we will look at tools and strategies you can use to change that too.

Many of us underestimate the importance of credit. If we were raised with an old-school mindset, we might feel that buying anything on credit is like spending money you don't have. Some of us avoid taking out lines of credit at all for that reason. But the reality is much more complex than that.

Those who read my first book, *The Credit Game: Plays We Were Never Taught*, know that credit scores affect far more than how much we can buy without paying up-front. Having a track record of securing and using personal credit responsibly can mean getting better prices, better interest rates, and more purchasing power.

In fact, the financial system is built to punish those who don't buy on credit: if you have no track record for paying back loans or credit cards, you will be considered a less reliable payer for any purchase or loan you might wish to undertake in the future.

The benefits of good business credit—and the consequences of not having it—are even more severe. Having a poor business credit score can mean paying higher insurance premiums, being denied loans and business credit lines, and getting charged high-interest rates that cost you over time. This can limit your business' ability to grow, and can even shut you out of the best markets entirely. Many major vendors and suppliers will not sell to businesses with poor credit scores at all because they don't want to risk their invoices going unpaid.[1]

So how do you build good business credit? The good news is, it's more about having knowledge than about having wealth. As with personal credit, knowing how business credit scores are calculated and what potential lenders and vendors look for in a business' credit history is more important than how much you spend. When you have this knowledge, you can know exactly what types of credit lines to seek, how to use them strategically, and how to grow your borrowing gradually so that you don't get in over your head with debt on an untested business.

We'll see exactly how the system works in this book, just like we did for personal credit in *The Credit Game: Plays We Were Never Taught.*

Business credit is just as important as personal credit in several ways:

- Businesses generally qualify for bigger loans and lines of credit than individuals. Businesses are assumed to have higher expenses and higher cash flow, so business credit lines can help a business to thrive when personal credit is not enough.
- There are laws in place to protect business owners and their families from catastrophe in the event of a business disaster. If you set your business entity up properly and choose the correct lines of credit, your personal credit score and your family's assets will be protected in the event of business bankruptcy or loss.
- When it comes to big purchases, some vendors and creditors may refuse to do business with you *at all* if your business credit score is poor or non-existent.
- It solves the cash access problem here in America for people who don't qualify for traditional bank loans and funding.

I cannot overstate the importance of building business credit to starting a successful business.

A study by the National Small Business Administration found that 27% of small businesses reported that they were struggling, or were unable to take advantage of opportunities for growth because they could not procure sufficient funding.[2] To ensure you can afford to grow when opportunities for growth present themselves, it's a good idea to start building your business credit *now* with small steps that will build up to credit you can draw on to produce major financing in as little as six months.

The following methods can also help qualify you for other major loans when the time comes.

In this book, we'll learn:

- What paperwork and registrations you will need to ensure your business is set up properly and eligible for the best business credit options.
- How to separate your business finances from your personal finances.
- How to build business credit using your Employer Identification Number instead of your Social Security number, keeping your personal assets and finances safe.
- The pros and cons of different types of business credit, and the types of business credit you must get if you want to have an optimal business credit portfolio.
- How to stack different levels of commercial accounts to avoid being a personal guarantor and to save the grief of multiple hard inquiries.
- How to become double, triple, or even quadruple lendable by applying these strategies to every business you own!

As you read this book, I encourage you to "do your homework" as you go along. We'll discuss quite a few pieces of paperwork you will want to file to set up a business entity that is eligible for a business credit score. This paperwork may get overwhelming if you save it all for the end of the book, but it will be easier to break down if you submit a few pieces of paperwork at the end of each chapter before moving on.

My goal here is to help you get it done, just like I did as a small business owner with limited capital. After discovering how powerful credit could be, I have dedicated nearly the last decade to learning everything I could about business and personal credit so I could help people to realize dreams they may never have been able to finance otherwise.

I invite you to read this book twice. Once all the way through, ensure that you know your big-picture strategy from start to finish; then again, chapter by chapter, as you complete the steps contained in each chapter.

You'll find that each chapter contains a number of specific steps that may take a few weeks or more to complete. Some also specify that you should wait two months before moving on to the next steps. But if you take persistent action, you can obtain at least $50,000 in six to twelve months, and maybe even sooner.

This may seem like a long period of time now, but when you have the capital you need to start or grow your business, you'll be glad and wish you started sooner. During this time period of building, your credit history will grow as you apply to creditors, and as reports of bills you have successfully paid on time register with the credit bureaus. Once your business credit has enough positive accounts reporting, it will be healthy and robust enough to take the next big steps.

If you complete all the steps contained in this book within six months or so, you will be in a position to successfully acquire capital and other forms of alternative credit and financing, even if you started out with no money and no business credit score.

You *can* finance your dream. You've just got to know how.

CHAPTER 1
YOUR BUSINESS CREDIT STRATEGY

This book is designed to guide you through the stages of building business credit without having cash flow, collateral, or great personal credit. The term "stages" here is important because, as with any career path, you've got to have a strategy.

Many publicly available sources of information on business credit do not fully explain that some types are riskier or more difficult to get than others, or that having certain types of credit lines in place *before* applying for others can qualify you for more funding and more favorable interest rates without being a personal guarantor.

The widespread lack of cash access and attention to strategy in online how-tos is one reason why so many business owners become frustrated after, for example, applying for a business loan and being rejected. Often, they have never been told that bank loans are one of the most advanced forms of obtaining business capital and that it's a good idea to build their business credit through other methods *before* applying if they want to be approved.

I will begin this book with the assumption that you have no business credit score. You may not yet have taken a single step toward making your business a reality, or you may be a long-time business owner who has been running your business out of your personal wallet because you weren't comfortable applying for business credit or loans.

In either case, we will move from the assumption that you have no business credit score to a position where you can realistically apply for and receive tens or hundreds of thousands of dollars in funding to grow your business at favorable interest rates. This can all be done without risk to your personal credit or assets using a system that worked for me as a first-time business owner.

I will warn you: there will be a lot of paperwork and a little bit of footwork. But as you complete every step in this strategy, you will see how you are establishing your business as a reputable legal entity with a solid financial track record that makes you an appealing client for a bank loan, business grant, and other sources of funding that can stretch well up into the six-figure range.

Let's take a moment to learn about some of the concerns you as a business owner need to be aware of when considering applying for financing. We'll cover some of the risks and trade-offs contained within different types of credit lines, and see why some types of business credit can be riskier for business owners than others.

Meet the Credit Bureaus

The arbiters of credit scores are a group of organizations called credit bureaus. These are private companies, but their jobs are considered so important that they are subject to regulations by the federal government to ensure that they do their jobs thoroughly and fairly. What exactly is the job of credit bureaus? It's to keep track of the "credit scores" of businesses and individuals.

Credit scores are designed to predict the future cash flow of businesses and individuals. This information is then used by vendors, credit card companies, banks, and other entities to decide how much money to lend an individual or business, how much interest to charge, and sometimes whether to do business with a company at all or whether the company seems too distressed or risky.

Because so many potential lenders and business partners will look at our credit scores to make important decisions about our businesses, it's important to understand who the major credit bureaus are and how to make sure the credit reports they put together about our businesses look great. Meet the most important business credit bureaus in the U.S.:

- Dun & Bradstreet. This is the "gold standard" of business credit bureaus by many people because it offers reports, not just on a business's credit history, but also on matters like its "business family tree," which shows a list of businesses with which a given business is legally or financially intertwined.
- Dun & Bradstreet is even experimenting with offering cybersecurity ratings to evaluate a company's risk of suffering a hack or other IT system failure.
- We will show you how to apply for a D-U-N-S number and establish your Dun & Bradstreet credit report in Chapter 2.
- Equifax business credit scores. Equifax is one of the Big 3 credit bureaus which compiles personal credit scores, and they offer business credit scores too. As in personal credit, Equifax is considered one of the most reputable and comprehensive business credit scoring agencies.
- Experian business credit scores. Like Equifax, Experian is considered one of the Big 3 players in both personal and business credit reporting.

Throughout this book, we'll learn how to use our knowledge of these bureaus to build business credit history to the point where we can obtain tens of thousands of dollars in business financing within six months!

DEBT VS. EQUITY

Capital moves in our economy in two forms: debt and equity. "Debt" is when you owe someone something which you are expected to repay later or face adverse consequences. "Equity" is the valuation of ownership, where someone has actually used their infusion of capital to purchase something, like ownership of your company or your assets.

Debt is the most commonly discussed form of capital in credit discussions, as it is generally the way that credit cards, loans, and other common types of credit lines function. However, investors and certain types of "secured" financing will actually trade money for ownership of your business or assets which they can take or sell or make legal decisions for if they so desire.

This is important because giving up equity means giving up...

CONTROL

One major reason people start their own businesses is a desire for control over their craft or their career. While some people start businesses with the specific intention of selling them to a wealthy buyer after the business has become profitable, most entrepreneurs want to be able to run their business their way for some time.

Having all the control means that you also have all the financial responsibility. If you give up some of that financial responsibility, such as by bringing on investors or taking out credit lines that are secured with your assets, you are giving up control. Anyone to whom you give equity in return for capital can have a say in how your business is run.

Even some bank loans may come with requirements that the

bank be allowed to review your business's financial performance and require changes as a condition of obtaining the loan. This is generally not a bad thing as the bank's only interest when lending money is the profitability of your business, and that's your interest too. Banks generally will not try to micromanage your business because their only concern is that you pay them back with interest.

Investors, on the other hand, are less restrained in what they can require of your business. This is why obtaining investors is generally recommended as the *last* step in your business financing journey, and some business owners choose to forego investors altogether.

SECURITY

Credit lines come in both "secured" and "unsecured" varieties. "Secured" lines of credit are those in which your lender "secures" their loan by having you sign legal paperwork stating that you will forfeit certain assets to them, or that they will be able to take certain types of action against you if you don't pay them back.

Be sure you understand what you are signing up to forfeit if you choose to pursue secured lines of credit. Are you willing to lose whatever you are promising if you can't pay this credit line back?

Secured credit lines can have advantages over some unsecured credit lines, such as sometimes having lower interest rates (the lenders' logic is that since they cannot really force borrowers to pay them back, they will charge all of their borrowers' higher interest rates to make up for the money they might lose from some through nonpayment). But there may be times when unsecured lines are better.

You may be beginning to see more examples of why it is so important to understand business credit strategy. New business owners who take on investors without realizing they are losing some control of their business, or who offer their home as an asset to secure a loan may find themselves in very unwelcome territory if their investor starts demanding changes to their business or they encounter problems paying off their secured loan.

TRANSFERABILITY & SEPARABILITY

Two big reasons to build business credit are separability and transferability. Both refer to the question of whether the capital or debt you obtain is yours personally, or belongs to your business.

For business reasons, it may be desirable to be able to transfer your business's financial assets, such as its credit history and its capital, to other owners. This may be useful, for example, if you decide to sell your business to a new business owner for a large lump sum of money when you retire, or if you have a business partner to whom you want to be able to transfer some financial duties.

It is also highly desirable to maintain your business capital and debts separate from your personal assets and your personal credit score. New businesses are inherently risky and ensuring that debts stay with your business, not with your personal credit score or your personal assets, means that you can protect assets like your home and credit score even if the worst happens to your business.

Generally, transferability and separability go together: if debts and capital are linked to your business as a separate legal entity, not to you personally, then you have the power to transfer them to future owners of your business.

EASE OF ATTAINMENT

Some types of credit are more readily given out than others. This may be because they are only small loans or credit lines and do not represent a large risk to the lender, or it may be because the consequences for failing to pay them back are so severe that the lenders have a high confidence that they will be paid back.

Both in personal finance and business, it's important to understand *why* it is easy to obtain any line of credit you are offered. Is it because it's a mutually beneficial situation for you and the lender? Or because the lender knows they will extract far more money from you in repayment than you are actually borrowing?

In my simple business credit-building strategy, we will focus first on lines of credit that are both low-risk and easy to obtain. This will allow you to start building credit history with relatively low risk. We will then move on to more exclusive and more challenging types of credit, allowing you to build your skills over the course of six months or so. This can be thought of as the fastest possible timeline for building your skills and credit using an optimal strategy within the confines of the business credit system.

In the four tiers I use to discuss business finances, lower-tier types of financing are generally those which are lower-risk and easier to obtain, while higher-tier types are either riskier or harder to obtain. The presumption is that as business owners master less risky types of credit and build credit history, they will develop the credit history and the skills they need to obtain and successfully profit from more challenging types of financing.

It's worth noting that the phrase "tiers" may be used in different ways by different parties in the credit and finance world. Experian, for example, uses "Tier 1 credit" to refer to the very *best* business credit which is accomplished through many years of work.[1]

I don't find this approach useful since it does not help business owners to build their credit step-by-step from the ground up, and specific credit score numbers can be used to more precisely understand one's chances of approval for new lines of credit. So in this book when we refer to "tiers" of business credit, we will also be referencing the following terms:

PERSONAL GUARANTOR

Most business owners know nothing about business credit and often use their personal credit to start or grow their business. Unfortunately, about 29% of businesses fail and end up costing business owners their personal assets, savings accounts, and personal investments in the process.

This book teaches an alternative way to master business credit so that it does not hold you, the business owner, personally liable for the business's debts and commitments. "No personal guarantee" means not risking your home or your vehicle, or having to mix finances.

Opting out of being a guarantor will also protect you from losing credit score points caused by multiple hard inquiries when applying for business credit lines, for example. This means you can continue to enjoy excellent personal credit and all the perks that come with it even as you rapidly open new lines of credit for your business.

TIER 1: NET TERM VENDOR ACCOUNTS

Nearly all businesses that buy supplies from vendors have some sort of basic trade credit. These are credit lines where vendors and suppliers agree to allow businesses to purchase supplies and equipment on credit and pay them back over time. These can include vendor credit, retail credit, and equipment leases that usually come with a net 10, net 15, net 30, or net 60 trade account.

"Net" here means the full amount of your invoice is due within the number of days specified. Net 10 or net 15 accounts must be paid off in as little as 10-15 days after your purchase or when the invoice is sent out, while net 30s or net 60s may afford more time.

To start building your business credit, I recommend using net 30 accounts. This is because these accounts offer a good balance of time and speed. Also note that in order to activate the majority of these accounts, a purchase anywhere between $50-$100 must be made for it to report to the bureaus.

Typically, payments are collected and reported to the credit bureaus every 30 days, which allows you to build up multiple positive payment reports from several vendors in just one month. But because net 30 accounts give you a full month to pay, the chances of you forgetting or being unable to pay are lower than if you were trying to pay off your accounts every 10 or 15 days. Remember, what you *don't* want to do is take out a line of credit and then forget to pay it back by the deadline!

Net 30 accounts are usually offered by vendors who sell specific business supplies. The highly specific nature of these credit lines makes them both easy to obtain and low risk. The vendor or supplier knows that you can only use their line of credit to buy from them, so you aren't going to go out and use the credit line they've given you on something else and subsequently fail to pay it back.

If you successfully use their supplies to make a profit and pay them back, you're extremely likely to continue buying from them in the future, so they will have gained a long-term customer. If you fail to pay them back, they can stop supplying you or repossess their equipment and take a relatively small loss.

This means that offering these trade credit lines is a good investment for the vendors and suppliers who offer them, so they are more eager to offer them to new businesses with little credit history than someone might be to offer a credit line that is higher-risk and less profitable to the lender like a credit card or a loan.

TIER 2: ADVANCED TRADE CREDIT

More advanced levels of trade or vendor credit are best for businesses that have spent a couple of months building up a solid history of successfully paying off their tier 1 net accounts. These advanced credit lines may allow you to borrow larger amounts and take more time to pay them back than with basic trade credit lines. They may also allow you to buy a broader range of products and look more impressive to potential business partners and creditors in your credit report.

That's good for your business if you are looking to expand and you want the ability to buy more supplies or equipment and pay for these items after you've expanded your operation and are profiting from them. But it can also be risky because if for some reason, you *don't* profit from the new purchases, you can be stuck, unable to pay the lender back a larger amount of money. In that case, both you and the lender face negative consequences.

You must not miss or have any late payments on these accounts, because building credit in this manner is solely based on payment history. This fact makes business credit much more unforgiving of these types of mistakes.

That's why these more flexible and expansive lines of trade credit are considered "Tier 2": they're best for businesses who have already learned to reliably turn supplies and equipment into profit by using basic trade credit lines for at least two months.

You may also be introduced to fleet credit in this tier. Fleet credit is used by companies like Amazon that have a fleet of vehicles. Although you don't have to have a "fleet" of vehicles, this type of credit line allows the ability to manage fuel costs and save on expenses such as vehicle maintenance.

TIER 3: REVOLVING CREDIT

As you continue to build your business credit history, you will apply for more challenging and more flexible lines of business credit after each milestone. Now that you have proven your ability to pay back your debts thoroughly using net-term accounts, it's time to look into tradelines that require more trust and offer more power.

Lenders may now be willing to offer you revolving lines of credit which do not require payment in full each month. For the purposes of our strategy, we are still using these tradelines primarily to maximize your business credit history so that you will become eligible for even bigger and better financing opportunities in the future. This means being conservative with their use, since having an impeccable payment history is vital to getting to the truly top tier of business credit and financing.

But this is also the point at which your new business credit lines can save you some serious cash on your business expenses, and allow you to do things you probably could not have done using personal credit alone. For this reason, it may be worth investigating which credit lines offer the best rewards programs and discounts for your business model, and considering that separately from the question of whether they report rapidly to the most desirable credit bureaus.

If you follow my directions, you will get to the point where you begin to become approved for these higher-end credit options within four months.

TIER 4: HIGH-LIMIT REVOLVING CREDIT

The last credit tier we'll discuss in this book will be high-limit and cash lines of credit. These are the biggest, most powerful, and most difficult to obtain business credit lines. They can include business credit cards with very high credit limits and very favorable interest rates and rewards programs, and other types of financing you may not have heard about before.

The risk-benefit trade-off here is obvious. A skilled business owner can do a *lot* with these lines of credit, and they show banks, investors, and other potential lenders or business partners that you are very good at managing your finances. But they also carry a high potential for both you and the lender to get into serious financial difficulty if you are given one of these highly flexible, high limit credit lines, and you spend money on things you aren't able to turn into profit.

Whether and when to apply for these credit lines will be up to you. My job here is to help you build the business credit score that will make this an option for you and to give you a chance to learn exactly how to turn credit into profit within your chosen business model as you learn to use safer and more modest credit lines along the way.

OUR 5-STEP BUSINESS CREDIT BUILDING SYSTEM

In this book, we will progress through the following steps:

1. Building your foundation by filing the appropriate legal documents to establish your business as a legal entity with finances separate from your own and which is eligible for its own credit rating.
2. Optimizing your business's financial profile to demonstrate to lenders that your business and its owner are reliable borrowers who will yield profit in the form of interest payments for anyone who lends to them.
3. Create and optimize profiles with the business credit reporting agencies, whose reports are used by lenders to decide whether to lend to a business.
4. Start vendor credit. This is a basic type of business credit that is often available with favorable terms relative to all-purpose credit lines. This will begin establishing your business's credit history as a reliable borrower with favorable payment terms.
5. Start revolving credit lines. This is another type of specialized business credit line that is broader in applicability and sometimes more challenging to manage. This makes it an excellent demonstration for future lenders that your business can handle multiple types of credit lines reliably.
6. If desired, at this stage you can also begin building cash credit by taking out more all-purpose business credit lines such as business credit cards. These can be useful to your business, but can also be more

challenging to manage because they have fewer restrictions and can be easier to overspend on. For this reason, I only recommend this strategy for those with healthy spending habits and a solid business plan.

So how can you take your business from concept to major financial player? Let's get started by procuring everything you'll need to obtain at least five to six basic trade credit lines!

CHAPTER 2
BUILD YOUR FOUNDATION

Starting a business can be intimidating, even if you're not thinking about credit and funding. The necessary legal and financial steps will vary depending on a business's industry, the city and state it operates in, and who runs it. Although some businesses can get away with far less paperwork than others, having specific pieces of legal paperwork in place makes it possible to build business credit which is separate from your personal credit and finances, not to mention making it easier to handle issues like legal liability and taxes.

A new business may need to:

- Legally register with their city, state, and local governments.
- Register as a legal entity such as a Limited Liability Corporation or an S-Corporation.
- Pay sales tax and/or business income tax.
- Create a business bank account.
- Apply for business loans or credit lines.
- Hire subcontractors or employees.
- Make legal and financial arrangements with suppliers, vendors, and partner businesses.

- Be prepared to deal with potential customer, employee, or subcontractor lawsuits.

This list deters many people from starting their own businesses, as many of these steps sound difficult or complicated. However, here I will show that they're not hard to do. We will go through the major steps necessary to set a business up for legal or financial success together.

I need to put a major disclaimer here: because laws vary by city and state, you should *also* consult your city and state's laws on these matters. I will share general information from a U.S. federal perspective, but the regulations for your city or industry may differ. Some states require more paperwork, licenses, and fees than others, and the same business may or may not need a license, depending on the city and state it is located in.

My goal here is to give you a good start so that by the time you go through these steps, performing any additional steps your city or state may require of you will seem easy!

HOW AND WHY SHOULD YOU REGISTER YOUR BUSINESS?

Registering a business means filing paperwork with your city and state to establish your business as an official legal entity. This is usually required in order to file taxes and procure business credit, as lenders and creditors need legal documentation proving that a business is an established legal entity before they can start reporting its credit score to credit bureaus and certainly before they will think about lending a business money.

Incorporating your business as a legal entity can also offer some protection against the consequences of bankruptcy and lawsuits, since these may be filed against the *business* as a legal entity instead of against the owners as individuals.

This is not a "get out of jail free" card—if a business owner can be proven personally responsible for legal or financial misconduct, they may still be the recipient of the consequences. But under other circumstances, the owner can be partially shielded from the consequences of circumstances beyond their control. This is especially true if the business owner purchases industry-appropriate liability insurance, which usually also requires that the business be legally registered in order for the insurance to be properly applied.

So what is the first step to registering your business?

NAMING YOUR BUSINESS

Your business's name is a big deal. It's the first thing a customer encounters when they learn about your business, and it will create their priceless first impression of you. It may also have surprising effects, such as affecting the amount of competition you face to get onto the front page of Internet search results, or determining how far down an alphabetical directory list your business appears. There are also terms and words that are wise to avoid, as many industries are considered high-risk and may result in a lack of funding opportunities.

When selecting your business name, consider questions like:

- Does this name communicate my personality and my brand's personality? If people are drawn to your personality, you want a name that communicates what that personality is.
- Is this name similar to the name of another popular or local brand? That may be a bad thing; your business may face a lot of competition for search engine rankings from that big brand, and customers may even get confused and buy from that other brand instead of from you.
- Could this brand be off-putting to your customers in any way? Some businesses find out too late that a term they used in their name is not viewed as credible or reputable by their audience.

- Is my business a high-risk industry? Avoid using terms like credit repair, trucking, real estate, accounting, cannabis, etc.

Keep these questions in mind as you begin brainstorming potential names for your business.

It's a good idea to start with what BigCommerce.com calls a "word dump." There are probably hundreds of words that could be relevant to your brand and industry. Each word sends a particular message and has a particular personality. Which words are right for your business name?[1]

Try using this checklist to ensure that you get all the juicy words that might apply to your business out on paper.

- Words about what your business does or produces (cookies, computers, lawn care, etc.).
- Words about the experience you want to give your customers (affordable, bliss, easy, power, premium, sweet, etc.)
- Words about any unique aspects of your business model (custom, delivery, rental, name of your town or city if you will serve mostly local customers, etc.).
- Words about the people who run your business (your names, experts, family, geeks, etc.)

Try to come up with a list of at least 100 words to mix, match, brainstorm, and sleep on. In the morning, come up with six to twelve names to ask family, friends, and members of your target customer demographic for their opinions.

Once you have a few favorite names in mind, you will want to check the following:

- Search state records to see if someone is already using this business name in your state. If they are, you probably will not be allowed to register a business with the same name. Each state should have its own name check tool, usually located at an official "state.gov" website. Using your state's official "state.gov" name check tool will help ensure that you are using your state's complete public records, and not a free search offered by a company that may have incomplete information.

- Search federal trademark records to see if someone else has already trademarked the name. These can be searched at: https://tmsearch.uspto.gov
- Check to see if the domain name "yourbusiness.com" is available. If it's not, that may make it harder to drive customers to your website, as they may accidentally end up at the other company's website instead.

Once you have found a name that you love and your target audience seems to like, and you have confirmed that its trademark and domain are available, you're ready to purchase your website domain. I recommend you do this right away, because although it is quicker, cheaper, and easier than registering your business as a legal entity, for all these reasons, a domain name is also more likely to be snatched up by another entrepreneur while you're doing your business registration paperwork!

Of note, most domain names should not cost much more than $20 per year to register. If you find that an unscrupulous business such as a domain "squatter" is demanding hundreds or thousands of dollars in exchange for your domain name, it may be worth contacting the company squatting on the domain to tell them that what they're doing is probably illegal.

"Domain squatting," or the practice of buying a domain and then demanding many times the domain name's market value from anyone who wants to buy it, is indeed illegal in the U.S. in most cases.[2] Some profiteers do it anyway, hoping that people will pay exorbitant prices for the domains they've acquired without realizing that the practice is illegal. If such a company fears a legal challenge, they may release the domain you are interested in back to market prices just to avoid potential legal trouble.

It's also worth noting that your name doesn't *have* to be "yourcompanyname.com." There is no legal requirement whatsoever around what your domain name must be. It's just that it's more likely that customers will try to get to your website simply by typing "yourcompanyname.com" without even checking what your official website domain is, so owning that domain is the best way to ensure that these customers can find you.

Once you've chosen your business's name and made sure you own your business's website domain name, what next?

OBTAINING A BUSINESS ADDRESS

During the process of registering a business, you will likely be asked for a mailing address to which your state will send important legal documents from time to time. In some states, this mailing address may also become a matter of public record in a searchable database. It's a good idea to search your own state's laws and determine if this is true for your state.

If you are concerned about your personal address becoming a matter of public record, here are some ways to obtain a business mailing address without having to make your personal address public or rent a whole office or storefront:

- Virtual office spaces are businesses that may provide mailing addresses, receptionist services, workspaces, and more to small businesses. This allows you to work from anywhere without having to take on the full cost of renting an office or storefront. The mail you receive may be forwarded to your residential address or may be available for pickup at a local location.
- UPS and the U.S. Postal Service are among the entities that offer rental mailboxes. These can include both standard P.O. boxes, and the USPS's "street

addressing" option, which allows you to give out the address of the post office where your P.O. box is located as a full mailing address.

- Some coworking spaces may also rent mailboxes out or offer address services.
- Assign a registered agent.

If you don't have a store or office space to use as a mailing address and you don't want your residential address to be listed as part of public record, procuring one of these options for your business prior to filing your articles of incorporation may be a good investment.

Once you've got your name, your domain name, and your mailing address, you have everything you need to officially create your business as a legal entity. Now, what kind of legal entity will you choose to incorporate?

CHOOSE A BUSINESS STRUCTURE

There are different business "structures" to which different laws about tax, liability and other matters apply. These different structures are designed to give different advantages and place different regulations on businesses of different sizes, with different numbers of owners and different types of business activities, etc.

It's a good idea to do further research about which business structure will be ideal for your business beyond just reading this book. Until you have a chance to do that, an extremely brief rundown of the most common types of business structures for new business owners is as follows:

- Doing Business As. This piece of paper allows you to do business under a fictional name, such as a pen name, a performer name, or a business name, without having to create a separate legal entity for that business. I do NOT recommend you use a DBA for our purposes because a DBA will not allow you to obtain the legal standing you need to build business credit. However, it is an option that can be confusing, so I wanted to clarify its purpose.

- Sole Proprietorship. Sole proprietorships are the default type of business you are running if you are running a business by yourself and have not incorporated another type of business entity. Freelancers and other self-employed people who don't work for a corporation are generally legally considered sole proprietors.
- This can make filing taxes easy, but sole proprietorships do nothing to shield the business owner from legal or financial liability. A sole proprietor's personal assets are not protected if their business should go bankrupt or be sued. This is why many sole proprietors eventually create an LLC or other corporation for their business.
- General Partnership. A general partnership is similar to a sole proprietorship in that it is the default business entity that is formed when two or more people start doing business together. In some places, a general partnership is automatically considered to exist if two people are doing business together, even if you haven't filed any paperwork.
- The drawbacks to a general partnership are similar to those of a sole proprietorship. Partners aren't protected from debt or liability, so their personal assets can be seized in the event of bankruptcy or lawsuit. This can be especially dicey because one partner can even be held responsible for business debts incurred by the other partner without their knowledge. This is another reason why LLCs are popular.
- Limited Liability Corporation. This is a common choice for new small businesses. Limited Liability Corporations are the simplest legal entities that offer

some legal protections to their operators and are eligible for Employer Identification Numbers, business bank accounts, business credit, and all the general perks and privileges of a corporation.

- Unlike other corporation types, LLCs generally do not require a board of directors or have strict rules about corporate proceedings.
- S-Corporation. S-Corporations offer certain benefits, such as tax advantages and the ability of the company to sell stock shares to investors. However, S-Corps are subject to stricter rules and regulations than LLCs and can only have up to 100 shareholders.
- C-Corporation. C-Corporations may be of unlimited size and have an unlimited number of shareholders. They are also subject to stricter oversight rules for this very reason. This is the preferred business structure for business owners who wish their company to go public on the stock market one day, but if that is not part of your business structure, it may be easier to avoid the added rules and regulations with an LLC or S-Corp.

Once you have decided which type of legal entity to create for your business, you will need to file paperwork with a state government to incorporate your new business entity.

Typically, this will be your own state. Most states require corporations to be incorporated and pay taxes *at least* in the state in which they operate, so in most cases incorporating in your own state is the safest and simplest thing to do.

You may have heard of some states incorporating in other states. California, for example, imposes an $800 tax on all businesses, regardless of their size or income, so some businesses look for ways to incorporate in other states. Delaware, by contrast, has a dedicated business court which is renowned for its speed and efficiency in deciding legal matters, so many corporations seek to incorporate in Delaware so that they can claim jurisdiction to use this court system if they should ever get into legal trouble or choose to file a lawsuit themselves. Some investors may even *require* that companies they do business with be incorporated in Delaware to ensure a speedy resolution of any business legal issues.

It is technically possible to incorporate in a state other than the one in which you live if you can find someone in that state to be your "registered agent" and receive important legal documents there.

However, realistically speaking, you will have to pay taxes and comply with the laws in both the state in which your business operates and the state in which it incorporates. So, unless you are looking for certain specific legal benefits only granted by some states, it may be safest and easiest to incorporate only in your own state to begin with.[3]

Your state's official "state.gov" website should have a section for business owners seeking to file articles of incorporation in the state. This should provide the paperwork needed to incorporate in your state.

Note that while many online legal services may offer to help you file your articles of incorporation in your state for a fee, it is not necessary to pay a company to help you with this. You can do so if you want the extra assistance, but any individual can fill out articles of incorporation for themselves and submit them directly to their state government.

OBTAINING AN EMPLOYER IDENTIFICATION NUMBER

Employer Identification Numbers are like Social Security Numbers for businesses. As the name implies, one major purpose of these is for use in record keeping related to paying employees and subcontractors. However, just like a Social Security Number, your business will also need one of these to prove its identity when applying for and building credit.

Like Social Security Numbers, Employer Identification Numbers are administered at the federal level. The official federal IRS website, IRS.gov, is the home of information about EINs and how to apply for them.

According to IRS.gov, the person applying for an EIN must have a valid personal Taxpayer Identification Number such as a Social Security Number or an Individual Taxpayer Identification Number. This is designed to ensure that you are real and that the EIN is not being applied for by a fabricated person or an alias.

Having any other information you may need, such as your business's mailing address, is also a good idea.

When you have your Taxpayer Identification Number and business mailing address on hand, you must apply for an EIN by filling out the IRS's online EIN application. The IRS website does not allow you to save your progress on this application, so it's a good idea to set aside some time when you can sit down at your computer and finish this application from start to finish.

Once the application is done, you will want to download, save, and print your EIN application confirmation screen for your records.[4]

You can also apply for an EIN by filling out and snail mailing paper forms to the IRS if you do not have a computer with an Internet connection, but these paper forms can take weeks to be processed by the IRS and can take much longer to correct if any errors have been made in the application. For this reason, I recommend filing online if possible.

Once your articles of incorporation have been approved by your state government and your EIN has been approved by the federal government, congratulations! Your baby business is now a legal entity eligible for its own bank account and business credit lines!

There are just a few more things you will want to have to build your image as a reputable company and ensure proper handling of your business finances.

OBTAINING A BUSINESS PHONE AND 411 LISTING

While it is technically and legally possible to use your personal phone as your business phone number, there are several reasons *not* to do this.

One is the risk of harassment: by using your personal phone number with your customers and clients, you are opening yourself up to receive calls from the public 24 hours a day.

The professional image of your business may also suffer if you answer business phone calls the same way you would answer personal calls, or if you mistake one for the other. Using a landline number instead of a cell phone is important to establish business credibility and national or international presence. It also gives you the ability to use the convenience of an interactive voice response system to direct your callers.

Lastly, if you want a business partner or employee to *also* have access to your business phone line, you don't want this to require that you give them access to use your personal phone unsupervised. It may become burdensome to be the only person who can answer the phone and take down messages for your business, and giving others access to your personal phone and voicemail may be even riskier.

Fortunately, there are a growing number of ways to obtain a business phone number affordably or for free. These include:

- Obtain a toll-free number from a phone provider. This will cost money just like any ordinary phone line would, but it can give you a professional toll-free number, or a custom vanity number that is easy for your customers to remember.
- Companies like kall8.com, Ring Central, Vonage, or your phone provider should offer options, including forwarding your business calls to different phones at different times and creating an automated menu to help direct calls to different people or departments.

If your business does not yet have the need or the budget for a traditional phone line, other options, such as a Google Voice number allow you to set up a free phone number which can be redirected to different physical phones, and free voicemail box which can be checked by different individuals via an online portal.

These free services are more limited in their capabilities than paid phone lines, but they may be useful for businesses which do not receive much phone traffic and which require flexibility in terms of who can make and receive business calls.[5]

Note that not all phone numbers which are registered with a phone company are automatically listed in the national 411 directory. It is important that you are listed in the national directory because this is what lenders will use to verify your business name, address, and phone number. Cell phones are not eligible to be listed in this directory which is another great reason to use a toll-free number. You can register your business with the national 411 directory at listyourself.net and wait about a week for it to be published before checking registration.

It's also important to note that Google Voice numbers are usually not eligible to be listed in 411 information directories. These phone numbers are classified differently from landlines or mobile numbers that are linked to physical phones. This is another reason to get a paid business phone line if possible.

WEBSITE & EMAIL

Remember when we purchased your business domain name? Now it's time to use it. We live in a digital age, and it is likely that most of your customers find and interact with their service providers primarily online. For this reason, it is vital that you have a professional-looking website which contains all the information and features your customers need to make it as easy as possible for them to decide to buy from you. Essential website features include:

- A landing page that gives customers a good idea of what you offer and makes it easy for them to learn more about—and be tempted to buy—your products and services.
- An email address collection feature that allows you to build a mailing list of people you can contact with special offers and news about new products and services. You may wish to offer a coupon or a useful free download, known as a "lead magnet," as an incentive for customers to give you their email addresses.
- A page of Frequently Asked Questions that answers the ten or so most common questions or objections that may stop customers from buying from you. Try to address whatever the most common concerns for customers in your industry might be.
- If possible, an online store allowing customers to order products or book services from you right on your website. If a customer can make an impulse buy online, they are more likely to come back to you again and again.
- There are many services available to help you do this, including services that arrange online retail shipping, services that allow customers to book appointments with you using an automated calendar, and services that coordinate local food delivery.
- Your hours of operation should be listed so that customers know when they can expect your business to be open.
- Your business phone number should be listed so that customers can call you with questions.
- If possible, an online live chat feature where customers can ask questions quickly just by typing a message. Some web hosts offer messaging services which will direct these messages to an app on your phone so that you or your associates can text back promptly without

having to pay a full-time customer support agent. Chatbots are a great option too.

- At some point you will probably want to invest in Search Engine Optimization to help you show up higher in search engine results. However, this doesn't need to be done right away if search engine results are not expected to be your major source of customers and sales.
- While you are making your website, it is a good idea to also make a Google Maps profile for your business. This profile will allow customers to find your business if they are searching for products or services in your industry near your geographic location. It will also allow customers to leave and read reviews, and give you a place to encourage people to post good reviews of your business.

These are just a few features that are helpful to have on your business website. None of them are legally required, but all of them will help you to build and engage your audience and make more sales.

There are many web hosts out there which offer different benefits for different types of businesses. However, to be honest, I recommend Squarespace, because it is affordable and makes it fairly easy to incorporate all of these features into a beautiful-looking website.

I'm not affiliated with Squarespace or anything—I've just found them to be the best mix of value and affordability for business owners who are new to web design. If you already know a lot about web design, you may have other preferences based on hosts which will allow you more affordability or more flexibility that you can make use of with your expertise.

OBTAINING A BUSINESS E-MAIL ADDRESS

Many website hosting packages will offer one or more email addresses with "@yourbusiness.com" as their domain. This can be a very good option since it gives your business the air of official credibility that comes with having websites hosted at your domain name.

You can create email addresses such as "info@yourbusiness.com," or "yourname@yourbusiness.com," depending on what will best suit your customer's needs and the image you want to project.

If you don't want to pay for "@yourdomain.com" email addresses, you can also make free email addresses using other services, such as Gmail or Google Workspace, to serve as the email address for your business. This looks slightly less professional since everyone knows that these addresses are free and anyone can make them, but there is nothing technically or legally wrong with using such free addresses and they may serve your customers just fine.

But whatever you do, don't go without a business website and email address. These are likely to be the most common way customers want to find and communicate with you, so you want to ensure you have these channels in place as soon as possible!

OBTAINING BUSINESS LICENSES AND PERMITS

I will be honest here: business licenses can be quite confusing. This is because different states and even different cities may have different requirements for what kinds of businesses need what kinds of licenses. The simplest way to determine what the requirements for your specific business are probably to search "what licenses do you need to operate a _____ business in <insert your city and state here>."

Almost all cities and states will require businesses with potential health or financial implications for customers and employees, such as food-related businesses, businesses involving the use of heavy machinery, cosmetic or wellness services, and certain types of accountants or financial advisors, to have some kind of license.

Some cities may require licenses for just about any type of business, such as San Francisco's requirement that all electronics repair businesses have a special license since there are possible safety hazards from incorrectly repaired electronics. Some businesses, like car washing and car repair, may require a business license in some cities but not others.

If your business has a physical location or uses certain types of supplies or machinery, there is a good chance you will also need a permit. Different kinds of businesses may need to meet different kinds of requirements for fire safety, safe disposal of potentially hazardous waste, safe handling of potentially hazardous chemicals, and more. Again, these requirements will vary by state.

It is especially important to make sure that you know the safety requirements for spaces in your industry *before* renting or buying an office or retail space. Business owners can end up in a tight spot if they buy or rent a retail space and then discover, for example, that it does not meet the local fire safety regulations for the type of products they plan to sell. These regulations can vary by industry, so a food service business may need a space with different fire safety ratings from a retail business.

The only way to know what kinds of licenses and permits your business will need is to research your city and state's specific requirements. Be sure that you know this information before you start selling goods or services, as the fines and penalties for operating a business that requires a license without one can be hefty.

This system may seem burdensome at times but try to have patience with it. Remember: all these licenses and permits are ultimately for the safety of customers, employees, and residents. You wouldn't want a business operating using toxic chemicals or fire hazards near your home without a license proving that they had met safety requirements, and you wouldn't want to do business with a professional "expert" only to find that they weren't actually able to pass licensure tests for their industry. So please ensure you meet all the requirements yourself as a responsible business owner.

BUSINESS BANK ACCOUNT

In order to obtain business credit and funding, your business will need to have its own bank account. Fortunately, this is easy to procure once your articles of incorporation and your EIN application have been approved by your state and federal governments. You will also likely need documentation of any business licenses that your city and state require for businesses in your industry, so that your potential business credit lines can verify that your business is legitimate and properly licensed.

Once everything is properly registered with the appropriate government agencies, your business will be eligible for the same kinds of financial accounts as you are, and then some. Types of accounts your business may need include:

- A checking account. This is an account from which your business can directly withdraw money to pay expenses.
- A savings account. This is an account where your business can save money for long-term goals that is not available for daily spending purposes.
- A credit card account. This is a line of business credit to which expenses can be charged.
- A merchant services account. This is a type of account used by businesses to *accept* payments from customers. Deposits can be made to this account through your payment methods.

Before opening your bank accounts, you will want to check the offers available to businesses through local banks. Although it may seem simpler to set up your business bank accounts through the same bank as your personal accounts, that may not always get you the best offer and all the features that would benefit your business.

When deciding what bank to use, compare features like:

- Any monthly fees these banks may levy on business bank accounts.
- Minimum balances that may need to be maintained to avoid bank fees.
- Interest rates you earn on money in your accounts.
- Interest rates you pay on money owed on your business credit card.
- Any transaction fees or termination fees to end your credit line.
- Introductory offers such as offers of signup bonuses or low interest rates.
- Rewards programs such as business credit cards that grant you points to buy things that are useful for your industry. Some banks may offer credit cards that offer specific types of rewards tailored to businesses in specific industries.

Once you have selected the bank that you believe offers your business the best deal, you will need to present the following documentation to open an account in the name of your business entity:

- Your business's EIN or other Tax Identification Number.
- Proof of incorporation if your business is, indeed, a corporation.
- Any business licenses or registrations required by your city or state.
- Proof of address for the address at which you plan to receive bank correspondence about your business.

- Proof of identification as the owner of your business, such as a driver's license, passport, or state identification card.

When you have your documentation gathered, it's time to go to the bank to open your accounts.

At this time your business will not have any credit history, but don't worry. We will add new business credit lines as we go and investigate potential upgrades to your existing business credit line throughout this book. Since your business is now an official legal entity, we can do it all without risking or harming your personal credit.

If you already have pretty good personal credit, minimal hard inquiries, and are confident in approval, this may be an opportune time to apply for a business credit card as a personal guarantor. This means that you may be asked to personally guarantee that you will repay money borrowed by your business.

This is a kind of business credit to be especially careful with. Don't take out loans or rack up charges you can't afford to pay back at this time, since this may affect your personal credit as the guarantor. But using this line of credit reliably to make and pay back small business purchases will allow you to start building business credit history immediately.

I probably don't need to tell you to use your business credit line and all your business accounts responsibly. Don't make personal deposits or purchases using your business accounts. This will ensure that you do not get taxed twice or fined by the IRS. Your personal and business finances should always be kept entirely separate.

If you plan to spend money your business makes for personal reasons, do it by paying yourself a "salary" from the business account rather than by charging personal purchases directly to your business bank accounts. Charging personal purchases to a business account could raise suspicions of embezzlement or fraud, and you don't want that!

Now that you have a business bank account, you are eligible

for other types of business credit lines that we will discuss throughout this book. These accounts will ask you to apply for credit using your EIN and may ask you to pay off your business credit lines using your business bank account.

Having a business bank account is the safest and easiest way to grow your business' credit score, since it is a wall of separation between your business and personal finances. This allows you to grow your business' credit score independent of your personal credit score and keep your business's money separate.

This independence protects your personal credit score and assets in case of bankruptcy, and allows co-owners and future owners of your business access to the benefits of your business's credit since these things are no longer dependent on your personal finances.

There is one last thing you will probably need to start and run a successful business. I cannot give you a comprehensive course on this subject in the space of just one book, but I want you to be set up to succeed so I am going to address it briefly.

Know that there are many courses on this final subject available to you online, and local organizations such as your local SCORE administration office may even be able to offer you free expert help with this last vital component.

This last vital component is your business plan.

WRITING A BUSINESS PLAN

In its simplest form, a business plan is a document where you write down exactly how you plan to make a profit from your business. This document will most often be requested by banks when seeking a business loan or certain other types of credit lines. It will also be requested by investors if you choose to seek those in the future. Its function is to help you create a realistic plan to optimize the growth of your business, and to prove to others that your business is worth investing in.

Nine common components of a business plan include:

1. An executive summary. Think of this as an "elevator pitch" telling people what's great about your business. Include your company's mission statement, a summary of the products and services it offers, and a broad summary of your financial growth plans. You may wish to draft an executive summary first, then revisit and rewrite it after you have finished the other components to update it with any discoveries you have made along the way.

2. A company description. This more detailed technical description should include components like your business's full registered name, its mailing address and phone number, and the names of key people on your team.

3. Be sure to highlight the expertise brought by each team member so you can show potential lenders and investors your business' unique expertise, and you can keep your team's strengths in mind throughout the rest of the business planning process. If different people own different percentages or shares of your company, include information about who owns what as well.

4. A section on business goals. These should include some specific short-term goals so that all lenders or investors will understand what their investments in your business will be used for.

5. These should not be financial goals such as "make X amount of money," but rather goals that will help you *bring in* cash flow, such as launching a new product or service line, opening a new location, or launching a new marketing strategy to drastically expand your customer base. Include specific numbers such as the number of new customers you hope to recruit or the anticipated revenue from your new product line or location.

6. Detailed description of products and services. Here you will want to get into the details and the math of how your company will turn a profit. Include the following details:

7. An explanation of how your product or service is delivered to the customer.

8. The pricing model for your products and services, including the cost to provide these and the profit margin when customers buy them.

9. A description of the customers you serve and advertise to.

10. Your supply chain and order fulfillment strategy.

11. Your sales and marketing strategies, and the costs and return on investment so far if these strategies are already active.

12. Your distribution strategy.

13. Any patents or trademarks your company may own or have in process.

14. Do your market research. Lenders and investors will want to know what sets your company apart from the competition, and who your company appeals to. You will want to research and discuss factors including:

15. Who is your target audience, and why will they buy from you rather than other suppliers?

16. Who is your competition, what do they do well, and what do you do better than them?

17. Any important details about your target audience, such as whether they are an underserved market or whether you have identified an unmet need.

18. Outline your marketing and sales plan. This will include any methods you may use to bring in new customers, including deploying sales professionals, visual attractions in your storefront window, coupons and special offers for first-time customers, using online or other paid ads that reach target audiences in their everyday lives.

19. Include components that convert new customers into loyal customers such as loyalty programs, a sequence of discounts or special offers to incentivize repeat sales, personalized offers and interactions to cultivate personal relationships with the customers, etc..
20. If you have already put some of these into practice, report on their return on investment so far. This is easy to track if you are using online ads with click-tracking and purchase-tracking, but may be harder to track and optimize for methods such as billboards or radio ads.
21. Perform a business financial analysis. If you are already making sales and already have data on profit-and-loss and return on investment, include this information here. If you have them, you will want to include metrics like:
22. Net profit margin.
23. Current ratio of your liquidity and your ability to pay debts.
24. Accounts receivable turnover ratio.

Using graphs and infographics may help to drive home any positive points about your business' finances.

If you don't know what some of the above terms mean right now, that's okay. But you will want to research them. They are useful tools for predicting and optimizing a business's profits, and the more of these tools you master, the more profit you are likely to be able to bring in.

1. Make financial projections. In a big way, this is the final and most important act of your business plan. Everything else has been building up to this.
2. Your lenders and investors will want to know with as much certainty as possible that you will be able to pay them back and provide a return on their investment. So here is where you must show that your business *will* make a profit.

3. I advise that you *not* be overly optimistic on this section. It may be tempting to do so if you are trying to entice investors or lenders, but this business plan is also for *you*. You will do better if you underestimate your earnings and subsequently find ways to cut costs and improve your profit margin than if you overestimate your sales and profit margin and spend more money than you make.

4. So be conservative here. If you want to make your financial projections as impressive as possible, do that by finding ways to *increase* your profit margins through optimization and innovation. Not by artificially pumping them up with dubious hopes and assumptions.

5. If you already have quarterly reports, use these to illustrate how much your business is making and how much you expect it to grow when new products, locations, or marketing strategies are added.

If you do not already have quarterly reports, project as accurately as you can what you expect your business revenue to look like based on a realistic projection of your costs, profit margins, and the number of customers served over time.

It is not unusual for new businesses to take losses in their first two years, so if you cannot show profit right away, that is not the end of the world. But you will want to convincingly show that you can create a substantial and growing profit margin within two years—for your sake and that of the banks and investors.

You can download sample business plans to help you see exactly what to do for free from the website of the U.S. Small Business Administration at:

https://www.sba.gov/business-guide/plan-your-business/write-your-business-plan

Whew! That chapter was a doozy. But after completing it,

you should have everything you need to establish a fully functioning business and begin building your business credit score.

Now it's time to talk about the bedrock of business credit: your business credit report. Just like with your personal credit, your business credit report is where all the information about your available credit and payment history will appear. It is the report that your potential lenders, vendors, and investors will consult when deciding whether doing business with you is a profitable proposition.

CHAPTER 3
ESTABLISH (AND FIX!) YOUR BUSINESS CREDIT REPORTS

It's an intimidating fact that banks turn away about 80% of all businesses that come to them looking for a business loan.[1] When this happens, it's usually because the bank is afraid the business owner will not be able to make a profit and pay them back. Even if you don't need or plan to take out a business loan, this reflects the harsh reality that financial professionals don't always expect businesses to succeed and grow.

The good news is the same measures that will give your business a great credit score can also help your business to grow in all aspects by ensuring a proper focus on profit and financial growth.

If you are seeking a business loan, following the best practices for building your credit score can help put you in the top 20% of most prepared loan applicants. The same steps also place your business among the most likely to succeed, not just because of the availability of loans, but because following these best practices will get you to rigorously manage your business's finances and profit margin.

You may know that in your personal life, your credit report is like a report card for your history of paying your bills. Having multiple open lines of credit with a stellar history of on-time payments will build up your credit score quickly, while any bill you don't pay may be reported to credit bureaus and harm your credit score.

Credit scores can be frustrating because the system used to determine them is arbitrary and even a little bit secretive. For example, no one knows exactly what formula the Fair Isaacs Company (FICO) uses to calculate business credit scores. However, we have a fairly reliable understanding of what actions will help or harm your business credit report.

This chapter is about building an excellent credit report so your business can obtain the best deals, interest rates, and loans to help you grow.

The importance of a good credit score to a business cannot be overstated. Just like your personal credit, your business credit can determine things like:

- Whether your business can be approved for business loans, and how long the approval process will take.
- What interest rates you receive on business loans—in other words, how much money you end up paying the lender for the privilege of taking out a loan.
- How much money you are authorized to borrow to grow your business.
- Which landlords are willing to rent office space and other properties to your business.
- Whether investors are willing to invest money in your business.
- Whether major vendors are willing to do business with you.

So who calculates business credit scores, and how are they different from personal credit scores?

THE FICO SMALL BUSINESS SCORING SERVICE

The FICO Small Business Scoring Service, or FICO SBSS, awards businesses credit scores of between 0-300. These scores are used to make important decisions: for example, as of this writing the U.S. Small Business Administration will only consider making loans to businesses with a FICO SBSS of 140 or above. Businesses with a credit score of 160 or above have the best chance of being approved for an SBA-backed loan.

For a new business owner, your personal credit score can serve as the foundation for your business credit score. Since a new business has no credit history of its own, its owner's personal credit score may be used to determine what lines of credit the business is eligible for. However, be aware that too many hard inquiries often hurt business owners in the long run and take a long time to either remove or fall off.

The statutory limit for hard inquiries to remain on a personal credit report is two years. Applying for your first lines of business credit with a personal credit score of less than 600 may not be the best decision. Business owners with lower personal credit scores may be subjected to higher interest rates and other unfavorable terms when applying for business credit—meaning you'll pay more back for each dollar of business credit you obtain. This can slow the growth of a business and can make financial problems in the future more likely.

Having a personal credit score of over 700 is ideal when applying for personally guaranteed funds. Business owners with scores in this range will most likely get the best credit and financing deals. This can have a major impact on how much startup capital you can raise, what your profit margin on that capital is, and more.

Note that I say "ideal" here because, again, personal credit score is not always *necessary* to this process. If you want to start building revolving business credit or obtain loans right away, you can apply for lines of business credit that require a personal credit score, especially if you are already cash-flowing.

That's why I advise that people looking to start building their business get their personal credit into good shape first or during the business credit-building process. If you struggle with your personal credit score, or just aren't sure about it, my first book,

The Credit Game: Plays We Were Never Taught, covers how personal credit scores are determined as well as some of the easiest ways to build your personal credit scores up fast.

This may be an especially good idea since having good personal and business credit may help you get the best options in the higher tiers of business credit which you will become eligible for four to six months from now if you follow the steps in this book. Working on your personal credit alongside your business credit will put you in the best possible position when this time comes.

Just be sure you keep straight which of your credit-building accounts are for your business and which are personal so there isn't any confusion at tax time!

Once you've taken the steps from Chapter 2 to obtain a stable business foundation, you are ready to start building up a business credit score that will make you eligible for bigger and better loans and credit lines, as well as protect your personal finances and help your business appeal to investors.

When determining your SBSS, FICO will look at factors including:

- The personal credit history of the business's owners.
- The business's own credit history if it already has a credit history.
- Business financial data such as the business's assets and liabilities, cash flow, revenue, etc.
- The amount of time a business has existed. Most new businesses fail in their first three years, so simply showing that you've been in business longer than that may be considered evidence that you know how to manage your business's finances. If your business is brand new, though, don't worry—the other measures we take will more than compensate for this.
- Any negative marks against the business's payment history, such as past liens or judgments rendered against your business for non-payment of bills.

It's worth noting here that FICO uses different processes for evaluating small, medium-sized, and big businesses. This is important because otherwise, larger businesses would have a huge advantage over small businesses due to their larger cash flows and larger assets.

Since FICO considers business size when making credit score determinations, a sole proprietor freelancer can have the same FICO score as Walmart if they play their cards right, and can be just as likely to get approved for a loan![2]

HOW DO YOU BUILD YOUR FICO SBSS?

Remember how we said that a business credit score of 140 was necessary to be considered for an SBA-backed business loan? Good news! A business owner with a stellar personal credit score and excellent business cash flow can obtain a business credit score of 140 even if they just started their business last month and have no prior business credit history.

This is encouraging for any small business owner who is intimidated by the thought of entering the business credit game. However, 140 is the very minimum business credit score that may qualify you for SBA-backed loans. To have higher chances of getting more loans with better interest rates and higher credit limits, you will want to build your business credit in much the same way you would build your personal credit. For new businesses, there are two major ways to do this:

1. Maintain your personal credit. Sole proprietorships and new businesses are especially vulnerable to taking credit score hits if their owner's personal credit score drops.
2. Signing up for new lines of credit such as net 30 accounts, revolving credit accounts, and more. Throughout the rest of this book, we will cover which account types to apply to over the upcoming months to maximize your business credit score.

3. Just be sure not to mix in any personal transactions. Using business credit cards for personal expenses is a huge red flag for the IRS and credit bureaus and may cause your business to be seen as too risky to lend to or invest in.

Just like with your personal credit, there are more ways to build business credit. Any loans your business eventually takes out will determine how reliable your business is as a lender.

Businesses with prior histories of successfully paying back loans are more likely to be granted bigger financing with better interest rates in the future. However, I recommend that business owners who are new to business credit use business credit cards to build up their business credit scores and optimize their business spending habits before applying for loans or other types of financing.

Net 30 accounts are a low-risk way of borrowing money and showing you can pay it back because you are in control of exactly how much you charge on your business credit card each month. You can charge just a small amount each month on multiple net 30 accounts, showing that you can handle multiple payments responsibly and so can be trusted with future larger credit lines and financing.

On the other hand, loans and cash credit often involve agreeing to pay a significant amount back to the lender monthly on a long-term basis. This can be a struggle for new businesses that are just establishing their customer base or aren't used to handling bills from lenders. So not only will a new business with less credit history likely be asked to pay higher interest rates on a business loan—newer businesses may struggle to pay off their loans or high-limit credit lines on time which can harm their business credit history.

Try working your way up to a business credit score of 160 or higher through the maintenance of excellent personal credit and the strategic use of business credit cards before you apply for a loan or another type of high-risk financing. The more practice you have paying off creditors and the higher your business credit score when you apply, the more likely you will qualify for loans with great interest rates that you can use to grow.

The FICO SBSS is one of the most widely used business credit scores, so it's a good one to start paying attention to first. However, other organizations also offer business credit reporting and these may also be useful for business owners to be aware of.

HOW TO FIX BUSINESS CREDIT

If your business already has some negative marks on its credit history, you can begin repairing those and establishing a positive credit history today. Some strategies for doing so are obvious, such as paying all your bills on time and in full to establish an excellent payment history. Other strategies, however, might not be so obvious. I want to share a few tips here.

Steps you can take today to improve your business credit score include:

1. Making payments in full and on time. This is the easiest way to avoid accumulating negative marks in the first place.
2. Reduce your debt on revolving credit accounts. "Revolving credit" refers to accounts where your charges and balance can change monthly. This typically means credit cards or other lines of credit where you can charge various amounts and pay various amounts each month.
3. Owing a lot in credit card debt or other revolving lines of credit can lower your business credit score. So, one quick way to raise it is to begin paying those debts off as quickly as possible, even if you are not technically required to do so according to the terms of the credit line. Remember, our goal here is to please the credit reporting agencies—not just the credit card company.

4. In general, credit reporting agencies will give higher scores to businesses that owe less than 20% or 30% of their credit limit on each line of credit they possess. For the fastest results, take some time to review your credit lines and determine the fastest way to pay off your debts so you owe less than 30% of your limit on each business credit line you have.

5. Once you have gotten each business credit line you have down below 30% utilization, work on getting them all as close to zero as possible. It's not bad to owe a little money, but the less existing business credit debt you have, the more flexibility you will have to pay future unexpected costs or growth costs. Your card companies will also be more likely to raise your credit limit after paying in full each month.

6. Rehabilitate past-due accounts. Did you know that you can often negotiate with creditors or submit disputes directly through the bureaus (recommended) to have negative marks removed from your business credit report? Creditors will not normally advertise the fact that they offer this, but if you ask, they are often willing to negotiate in exchange for payment. However, disputing with the bureaus is often a lot quicker and easier than dealing with creditors.

7. Creditors want to get paid first and foremost. For that reason, they might agree to update their reporting to credit scoring agencies to remove negative marks if you make a certain number of payments in full and on time moving forward. This arrangement, sometimes called "pay for delete," which is just that. You pay the creditor in exchange for the deletion of negative marks from your credit score.

8. Open new credit accounts. Having a larger number of credit lines can improve your credit score by showing that you have existing sources of money to borrow from to pay off any new lenders.

9. Don't just spam business credit providers with applications—applying for a new line of credit usually results in your score losing a few points, so applying too many lines of credit in a short span of time is a bad idea. But by strategically applying for credit lines that you are likely to qualify for, you can increase your number of open accounts over time. The more credit accounts you pay off on time each month, the faster your credit score will rise.

10. That's why I recommend that when you obtain a new line of credit, you charge a small amount to that credit line and pay it on time each month. This is easiest if you set the credit card to autopay so that it will automatically be paid off in full each month without you having to manually remember to pay your bill.

11. Add positive trade references to your Dun and Bradstreet account. Not all vendors, suppliers, or business partners automatically report their information to credit reporting agencies. Some creditors often only report to bureaus when there's a problem, and that means these agencies might not know about all the on-time payments you've made.

12. Fortunately, Dun and Bradstreet allows you to report your own accounts, such as accounts with suppliers, vendors, and business partners, for inclusion on their report. In this way you can get credit for the on-time payments you're already making and improve your Dun and Bradstreet Paydex score.

13. Keep personal and business finances separate. It can sometimes be hard to adjust to using different payment methods for personal vs. business expenses, especially if you are used to paying your business expenses out of your own pocket. But it's essential that you keep these finances separate for several reasons.

14. Mixing personal and business finances is a huge red flag for the IRS. Using business funds for personal

expenses and confusing personal expenses for business deductions can be considered fraud, or even embezzlement. Though there's a clear moral difference between intentionally embezzling large amounts of funds and accidentally using the wrong credit card for personal expenses, the legal ramifications can be the same.

15. Mixing business and personal finances can also put both credit scores at risk. Your business credit score may suffer due to personal expenses being posted to your business account, which can make it harder to secure business deals and funding in the future.

16. You can seek a secured bank loan if all else fails. If your company badly needs funds or new credit lines to raise its credit score and it doesn't qualify for an unsecured loan, you may still be able to obtain a secured loan to keep the lights on and build up a successful payment history.

17. A "secured" loan is a loan where the lender knows they will recoup what they have paid you because you have promised to forfeit assets to them if you are unable to pay them back any other way. You may be able to offer assets such as a car or property you own as collateral, forfeiting ownership of these assets to the lender in the event you can't pay the loan back.

18. Obviously, this is something to be careful with as it can put your personal assets at risk. But it can also serve as a last line of leverage if you need to get a loan on record in order to build up your payment history and you can't get an unsecured line of credit. But before agreeing to it, make sure you can pay off this secured loan without going further into debt that may harm your credit history.

19. Business tradelines are another great option that are similar to being added to someone else's personal credit card account as an authorized user only for the

business. Depending on the source, these accounts can give a good boost and be temporary to permanent.

As you can see here, there are several ways you can add positive credit history to your business credit reports, and there are even ways to remove reports of late payments you've made in the past. But, what can you do if negative marks on your business's credit report don't even rightfully belong to your business?

ADDRESSING MISTAKES ON BUSINESS CREDIT REPORTS

Unfortunately, as with personal credit reports, errors and identity theft can also happen with business credit reports. The chances of this can increase if you accidentally provide incorrect information to a bureau, such as an incorrectly spelled name or an incorrect Employer Identification Number. They can also increase if other individuals or businesses have the same name as yours, leading to potential confusion of identity.

These incorrect items can have severe impacts on your business's prospects. Incorrect reports of unpaid bills, legal actions against your business, or other negative items can make it harder to find lenders, investors, vendors, and office space. How can you fix these problems on your business credit report if you have no control over the unpaid bills or negative actions that are being incorrectly reported as yours?

Every credit report provider is legally required to have a process to allow you to dispute incorrect items on your report. The dispute process is designed to remove incorrect items so that business credit reports are accurate.

In theory, this dispute process is generally simple and involves contacting the scoring agency which put the inaccurate item on your credit report. In practice, however, in some cases it can be quite complicated and difficult to get the mistake corrected. Credit scoring agencies may be reluctant to admit to mistakes or to expend the time and effort to comb through records to verify your claims.

Just as in personal credit, there is a science to disputing errors on your business credit reports. This science involves knowing the law around what credit reporting agencies are legally required to do for you, and demonstrating to them that you know the law. The dispute process may require contacting the agency multiple times over the course of months and using specific legal language to demonstrate that you know the law and will legally pursue the matter if the agency doesn't take appropriate action.

This is one area where my business, Major League Credit & Lending, can offer advice and assistance. A big part of our job is knowing the laws around credit reporting and using that knowledge to help clients to remove erroneous items from their business credit reports. Paperwork is also key to proving your case, so always keep an organized paper trail in the event that you may need to pursue legal action.

I will share some tips for managing this process throughout this book, but successfully disputing credit reporting errors can get sufficiently complicated that I could not fit all of the possibilities and recommended courses of action into this book. If you encounter a credit reporting error and do not have success in your initial attempts to get it corrected, don't hesitate to reach out to me to see how I can help.

CHAPTER 4
BUSINESS CREDIT TIER 1: NET 30 ACCOUNTS

Now that you've set your business up as an independent entity with its own credit score and credit reports, it's time to secure your first business credit. I recommend doing this by establishing your first store account with a vendor or supplier.

Store accounts are low-risk for borrowers and lenders alike precisely because they are restricted to buying from only one store.

For you, this means that you are unlikely to spend huge amounts of money and find yourself struggling to pay it back. If you can only use this line of credit on certain items necessary to your business's operation, the risk of budgeting errors or spending money on items that do not have a direct benefit for your business is low.

This, in turn, means that the creditor is less likely to lose money from nonpayment. The creditor is also likely to make more profit by selling you more products over time if they know that you have a special arrangement to buy supplies your business needs from their brand. They win customer loyalty and you win store credit. Everybody wins.

As we mentioned earlier, these come in different varieties, including net 10, net 15, net 30, and net 60. The number in these designations refers to the number of days you have to pay for the purchases you make using these lines of credit. I recommend starting with net 30 accounts to grow your business credit with the best mix of speed and reliability to ensure that your scores are reported to credit bureaus every month while minimizing the chances that you will forget to pay on a payment time.

These lines of credit may seem unimpressive at first glance. Obtaining a line of credit to buy shipping supplies, coffee cups, or car parts may feel less glamorous than obtaining a five- or six-figure bank loan. But that's exactly the point: these lines of credit are easy for anyone with a legal business entity to apply for, and they serve as the proving ground for later more challenging approvals.

Loans also, of course, help you to build your business. When you're first learning your business model and discovering what will be most profitable for you, you don't necessarily want to be making big money moves at that point. You are more likely to get the best possible return on your investment if you do your major spending *after* you have determined how to optimize your profit through trial and error in the early months or years of your business.

For their part, banks and other potential creditors are likely to reject someone with a brand-new business and no credit history who asks for tens of thousands of dollars, but they'll sit up and pay attention if a business owner who already has a history of paying off thousands of dollars per month in trade credit for six months or more offers to pay them *back* tens of thousands of dollars with interest.

When you have an excellent business credit score, banks will have high confidence that you will pay them back, and they may even compete with each other by offering you lower interest rates than the competition.

How do you even find vendors or suppliers offering store credit?

BEFORE YOU APPLY

Before you apply for trade/vendor credit, there are a few things you want to know to ensure that you get the desired result.

One thing to know is that it is very, very important that you register for these trade accounts using your business' registered name, EIN, and contact information. This is because the information you use to register your trade accounts will be the information that is also used to verify your business and report to the credit bureaus. For this reason, if you register under a personal name or if there is an error in the business information you submit, your activity on these accounts may not show up on your business's credit report. Any inconsistencies in your business information can also cause you to be denied financing, so make sure everything matches up across the board.

It's also useful to know that only $50 or more charges are reported to credit bureaus in most cases. That means you will want to spend at least that much on each of your tradelines to initially activate them and use them every few months if you want to build a strong, consistent reporting history.

You will also want to look for lenders with favorable terms. So what does a favorable line of trade credit look like?

ATTRIBUTES OF A GOOD LENDER

When opening a tradeline, you should be given information about its net/credit terms. This refers to the term you have to pay your tradeline lender. If you see the term "net 30," for example, that means that you have thirty days to make the agreed-upon payment to your tradeline lender. "Net 60" can mean you have 60 days, and "net 90" means you have 90 days.

Some businesses prefer longer net terms to give them more time to pay off their balances, but it's important to keep in mind that payments are only reported to the credit bureaus as often as they're made. This means that an account with Net 30 terms will report your successful payments to the credit bureaus faster and more frequently than an account with net 90 terms, which may not report your successful payment to the credit bureaus until 90 days after your first purchase with them. Some companies may even offer your business a discount on supplies if you pay your invoice early, so keep an eye out for rewards that could help your dollar go further as a small business!

Knowing when the 30 days you have to pay your invoice begins is also a good idea. When is the start date of this period? Is it the day you make the purchase? The day you receive a digital copy of the invoice? The day an invoice sent via snail mail is postmarked? If you plan to pay your balances early, you may not need to worry about this too much, but it's good information to have and to put into your business calendar to prevent any possibility of accidentally paying late.[1]

For this chapter, we will focus on vendors with two attributes ideal for businesses seeking to build Tier 1 credit history rapidly. These three important attributes are:

1. Net 30 accounts. While some businesses prefer longer or shorter payment periods, net 30 accounts are a fast yet reliable way to build credit history as they report your successful payments to credit bureaus just 30 days after they issue your invoice.
2. Report your payments to at least two of the three major business credit reporting agencies. All the vendors we will recommend here report your successful payments to at least two of the following: Dun & Bradstreet, Equifax, and Experian.

Some examples of businesses that offer reputable tradelines with favorable terms include Wayfair,[2] Quill, and Office Depot.

Quill, for example, specializes in helping new businesses build credit quickly with net 30 terms on a huge variety of items ranging from office supplies to laundry detergent to snacks and hot drinks for the break room.[3]

Office Depot offers a number of credit options for businesses, including a variety of rewards and payment terms which readers can view by following the link in this footnote.[4]

Uline offers tradelines that can be used to purchase supplies, including shipping supplies, packaging materials for retail products, and safety and janitorial supplies.[5]

Grainger is another favored tradeline partner for small business owners, offering tradelines that can be used to purchase tools and supplies for a variety of hardware-intensive industries, including HVAC, plumbing, lawn care and landscaping, laboratory equipment, metalworking, and vehicle maintenance.[6]

You can find many more vendors offering net 30 business credit lines for businesses with little credit history, but these are a few of my favorites.

There are also other resources to help you rapidly build business credit. Here are some other potential good additions to your early business credit portfolio.

ECREDABLE

eCredable is a company that will allow you to report almost any business account to Dun & Bradstreet, Equifax, CreditSafe, Ansonia, and Experian business reports as positive payment history. This can help you rapidly grow your business credit history without requiring you to make new purchases or spend more money.

With a $50 initial setup fee and about $10 per month fee thereafter, eCredable does cost some money but is arguably a good value for the ability to report thousands of dollars in preexisting bills to these major credit bureaus as credit history each month. You can explore eCredable's options and sign up if you wish using the link in this footnote.[7]

To me, eCredable is an obvious choice for businesses since it allows you to get business credit payment history for potentially thousands of dollars per month in bills you are already paying to landlords, utility companies, and more without needing a high-limit credit card you can charge these items to.

CREDITSTRONG

CreditStrong's business options allow new businesses to take out an interest-free loan for the sole purpose of repaying said loan on time to build credit payment history, which is then reported to credit bureaus. Businesses can borrow $2,500, $5,000, $10,000, or $25,00 and pay anywhere from $100 or $1,100 per month to build loan repayment history without having to qualify for a conventional bank loan.

While CreditStrong's loans are interest-free, they do charge a one-time "administration fee" to set up. This is how they protect their investment: since they are open to new businesses with little credit history, they must assume that some percentage of their borrowers will not successfully repay their loans, so they must protect their cash flow somehow.

For this reason, CreditStrong may not be right for businesses with very tight budgets or those concerned about their ability to repay a loan. But for businesses seeking to build credit history quickly and who have high confidence in their ability to repay the loan amounts in addition to their existing bills, CreditStrong can be a good option to qualify for a loan payment history without needing the credit history to qualify for a conventional loan. Interested parties can view their plan options using the link in the footnotes.[8]

NAV BUSINESS CREDIT SCORES & REPORTS

NAV is a little bit like CreditKarma for businesses. It offers credit monitoring and recommendations for business credit cards, equipment financing, merchant cash advances, and loans your business may qualify for.

I want to note that one should exercise caution when using both Credit Karma and NAV: both sites may be rewarded by creditors for referring borrowers, so not every recommendation they make will be in your best strategic interest. NAV may include lenders encouraging you to borrow more money than you can pay back, or offering you unfavorable terms such as high-interest rates. That's why it's important to read all terms and conditions, carefully plan based on your current cash flow, and be educated about good and bad terms on business credit lines.

That said, if you know the time has come to add a particular type of credit line to your business credit portfolio, NAV can help you find and compare options you qualify for. NAV also offers services, including helping small businesses apply for grants that don't need to be paid back, helping procure business insurance, and assisting with payroll and accounting.

If you have any questions about this process, my team of advisors at Major League Credit & Lending is here to help with a complete business credit-building system.

CHAPTER 5
MONITOR BUSINESS CREDIT REPORTS

Now that you have established your business's credit reports and obtained your first lines of business credit, it's time to think about monitoring your business credit. By monitoring your business credit reports, you can see what lenders see when deciding whether to lend to you—and ensure that what they see looks good.

STEPS TO CREATE A STELLAR CREDIT RATING

Your credit history is the most important component of creating a stellar business credit report. If you do perform all the following steps, there is a good chance that your business credit score will grow and thrive. To build amazing business credit, you will want to:

1. Open more than one line of basic trade credit. This allows you to be documented by credit bureaus as paying multiple bills on time each month, rapidly building your business credit score.
2. Keep your utilization rate low. Just like with personal credit, it's a good idea to charge less than 20% or 30% of your total credit limit on each line of trade credit

you have. This demonstrates that you have a lot of "wiggle room"—a lot of credit you can take advantage of if an emergency should ever interrupt your business's cash flow.

3. Pay your bill on time each month. Every on-time payment you make counts favorably toward building your credit score, while late payments can quickly harm it. Build your business's cash flow so that full on-time payments are a matter of routine and watch your business credit score grow.

HOW AND WHY TO MONITOR

If you do all the above each month, your credit score should grow steadily and eventually become excellent. However, there are a number of reasons it's useful to monitor your business's credit reports regularly. These include:

- Business credit reports don't *just* report your credit and payment history. As mentioned, some business credit reports also report your overall revenue and cash flow, your business's "family tree" of related businesses, and other factors related to your business. All of these factors can be optimized, and all are important to be aware of when planning to apply for new credit.
- Some of these factors, such as your business's family tree, may also change without your knowledge due to the actions of your business partners or their affiliates, and that is important to be aware of.
- The potential for error. Whether it's a credit bureau reporting something incorrectly, fraud arising from a malicious actor getting access to your company's business credit line, or an error with the submission or processing of your monthly payment, it's a good idea

to monitor your credit reports in case any errors occur that need to be corrected.

- Are you growing fast enough? Factors such as your credit mix (the mix of different types of accounts) can affect how fast your credit grows, so it's worth keeping tabs on how *fast* your credit score is rising to see if its rate of growth is meeting your expectations. If not, you might look at what types of accounts you lack that could speed things up.

So now that you've started to establish business credit, it's a good idea to check at least some of your credit reports on an at-least-quarterly basis. Many services also exist which will notify you daily, weekly, or monthly of any changes to your credit report.

It is also important to know that signing up for a credit monitoring service generally does *not* adversely impact your credit score. While making a "hard inquiry" about your credit in pursuit of opening a new credit line may temporarily hurt your score, routine credit monitoring services do not have the same effect.

Both free and paid credit monitoring services are available. Paid services may have advantages such as increased frequency of alerts, greater accuracy, and may include added features. Fraud, identity theft insurance, and monitoring of the dark web to see if your information has been leaked by hackers are two common services offered by paid credit monitoring services.

For my money, if you can pay a few dollars per month for tens or hundreds of thousands of dollars in identity theft insurance, that's a good investment.

So which credit reports should you monitor, and why?

DUN & BRADSTREET

As we've discussed, Dun & Bradstreet is a useful report for creditors and business owners because it provides a comprehensive picture of a business's health. Even beyond monitoring for errors and fraud, this is an excellent report to examine if you're looking for ways to improve your business's overall well-being and future prospects.

Once you have established your Dun & Bradstreet report, you will have access to useful pieces of information like:

- Your PAYDEX score. This number from 1 to 100 indicates your level of risk of paying your creditors back late or incompletely. The higher your score, the better Dun & Bradstreet thinks you will be at successfully repaying loans and credit lines on time. Scores over 80 are considered excellent and give you a high chance of obtaining success and low-interest rates when applying for almost any kind of business financing.
- Your delinquency predictor. This is a number from 1-5 which reflects your likelihood of paying a bill very late or not at all. In this case, a lower number is better: a score of 1 indicates a very low chance of delinquency, while a 5 indicates a very high chance of delinquency. Creditors want to be paid back on time, so businesses with a score of 1 are most likely to get access to the largest credit lines with the most favorable interest rates.
- Your financial stress score. This number is designed to predict the risk that your business will go bankrupt or close its doors in the next 12 months.
- The scores range from 1001-1875, with lower scores being better. Dun & Bradstreet will also sort you into a "class" from 1-5, with class 1 having the lowest risk of bankruptcy or closure, while businesses in class 5 have the highest risk.

If you see your business classified in class 4 or 5 on financial stress, it's time to make some serious changes to your business's cash flow before it's too late!

- Your Supplier Evaluation Risk, or SER rating. This number is designed to predict the risk that your business may cease operating or become inactive in the next 12 months. This particular number is used by businesses who may wish to hire your business as a supplier of parts and services to learn how likely your business is to continue supplying parts and services without interruption.
- SER ratings range from 1-9, with 9 representing the highest risk that your business will be unable to reliably supply parts and services, and 1 representing the lowest risk.
- Your Credit Limit Recommendation. This is a dollar amount representing the maximum amount of credit Dun & Bradstreet would recommend that a lender lend you. This may be used to determine the credit limit on your new credit lines, or the size of any loans you may receive.
- Dun & Bradstreet Rating. This is an overall score based on your company's size, industry, financials, and other factors. Higher scores indicate that a company is more likely to be successful in the long-term and is more likely to pay back its creditors.
- D&B Viability Rating. This is a performance rating that predicts the likelihood that a business will file for bankruptcy, cease operations, or close its doors completely within the next 12 months.
- D&B Cyber Risk Rating. This is an evaluation of how likely cyber threats are to interrupt your operations. This is based on factors like your company's degree of data and network security, and the extent to which your company's operations and finances depend on these computer systems to continue functioning.

I know—that's a lot of numbers and ratings! Each one is calculated based on a slightly different set of factors, drawn from Dun & Bradstreet's analyses of business performance over the years.

Different D&B scores are used by different potential business partners for different purposes. Consider which moves your business might be most likely to make in the near future when deciding which scores to consider optimizing.

Will you be seeking a loan or a major credit line in the near future? Then it might be wise to optimize your PAYDEX score, delinquency predictor, and credit limit recommendation. Will you be seeking to be contracted with other businesses to supply parts or services? Then you may wish to research how to optimize your SER rating.

MONITOR BUSINESS EXPERIAN

Experian is one of the major players in both personal and business credit. Although you might recognize it as one of the major bureaus you monitor for your personal credit, its business credit scoring system is quite different.

Once your Experian credit report has been established, you can check it through Experian or through other credit monitoring services. Your Experian credit score will be a number from 1 to 100, with an Experian business credit score of about 75 indicating excellent odds of approval for business financing and favorable terms on items including credit cards, loans, and certain types of insurance.

MONITOR BUSINESS EQUIFAX

Like Experian, Equifax is a major provider of business and personal credit reports. It is considered one of the top three, along with Dun & Bradstreet and Experian. Like Dun & Bradstreet, Equifax provides several numbers to help potential lenders and buyers rate your business's reliability. These include:

- Equifax payment index. This measures the total amount of your business's past payments that were made on time. Like Dun & Bradstreet's PAYDEX score, it is measured on a scale from 0-100, with a score of 10 or lower being good.
- To improve this score, ensure that all your business's bills are paid on time and in full every month.
- Equifax credit risk score. This score ranges from 101-992 and attempts to predict how likely it is that your small business will become severely delinquent on payments. A score of 892 or higher is considered good.
- It takes into account variables like your current credit utilization rate, your business size, the number of transactions your business has paid late, and the total age of your business's credit. To improve this score, keep your credit utilization rate low and your payments on time.
- Equifax business failure score. This score ranges from 1,000 to 1,600. Scores near 1,000 indicate a high chance that a business will fail in the near future, while scores near 1,600 indicate a high probability that your business will continue to exist for the foreseeable future. A score of 1,400 or higher is considered good.
- This score considers factors including the amounts of your business's recent debts, credit utilization rate, overall credit age, and delinquent bills. Pay down your debts, lower your credit utilization, and pay any delinquent bills to improve this score!

REQUEST A LEXISNEXIS REPORT

LexisNexis is another major provider of business credit reports. LexisNexis uses AI to search Internet databases for information including credit and legal records. These reports can include more detailed information, including records of such activities as property purchases.

LexisNexis is legally required to provide you with a free copy of your credit report from their files. Unfortunately, it doesn't always like to do so. LexisNexis has been known to occasionally refuse to send people free reports, claiming that they did not provide sufficient verification to prove their identity.

For this reason, it is recommended that you order your Lexis-Nexis report via registered mail, or with a return receipt request, to ensure that your request for your report and your report itself are both safe, secure, and thoroughly documented. It is also recommended that you keep a date stamped copy of your request.

If LexisNexis doesn't want to provide your free report, it may be necessary to cite your copy of your request and your return receipts proving that LexisNexis did receive your request as evidence to push them to send you your report.

LexisNexis will also request the following types of identification to prove that you are yourself and are therefore entitled to a free report on yourself:

- Your government-issued photo ID, such as a driver's license or state ID card.
- A current bank or credit card statement providing proof of your current address.
- Your Social Security Card.

For more information about how to access your LexisNexis report, you can visit the website listed in this footnote and its associated links.[1]

REQUEST YOUR CHEXSYSTEMS REPORT

ChexSystems is another type of report that most banks and credit unions look at when verifying an individual and a business as a potential account holder.

A ChexSystems report contains information about bank accounts, the history of delinquent accounts, and more. Inaccurate and negative information on these accounts can have a negative impact on your business, as banks, credit unions, and other financial institutions may be reluctant to do business with you.

For this reason, we recommend that business owners request a copy of their individual and business ChexSystems report at least once a year. This protects against errors and surprises that may be costly when applying for a bank loan or making another major financial move. You can request your ChexSystems report using the link in the footnote below.[2]

WHAT TO DO IF YOU SEE A PROBLEM

If a problem appears on your credit report, the correct approach to fix it will depend on the type of problem.

Problems with late payment, cash flow, and other attributes of your business are relatively "easy" to fix by filing a simple dispute. It's also important to optimize your payment history and cash flow, not just to please credit reporting agencies, but because constant improvement to these metrics is good for the overall health of your business.

But what if a negative mark appears on your credit accounts, and it's *not* because of something you or your business has done? What if you suspect fraud, identity theft, or a reporting error?

The first sign of fraud or identity theft is often unauthorized charges on your credit accounts. If you discover charges on your business credit account that you didn't authorize, the first thing to do is to freeze your credit accounts. This freeze will prevent new charges from being made to these accounts, protecting you from any further unauthorized spending.

Some credit lines may allow you to freeze *only* new or unexpected transactions while continuing to allow your routine monthly payments to go through. This can be useful for allowing you to conduct business as usual while protecting against fraud.[3]

Another way to discover fraud, identity theft, or a credit

reporting error is to notice a change on your credit report that does not match your expectations from your payment history.

When this happens, it's a good idea to first check the relevant account to ensure that the credit report doesn't reflect financial activity you didn't know about. A forgotten unpaid bill or a failed autopay can occasionally result in late payments or nonpayment even though you thought your payment history was up-to-date.

If the credit report issue involves blatantly incorrect information or credit accounts that don't even exist as far as you're aware, you may be dealing with identity theft or erroneous reporting. In this case, you will want to file a dispute with the credit bureau to have the incorrect or fraudulent information removed.

Sometimes, filing a dispute successfully is as simple as using the "dispute" feature on the credit monitoring agency's website. Unfortunately, other times the fraudulent or mistaken information *looks* accurate, so the credit bureau may refuse to remove it from your report initially.

When initial attempts to dispute an error on your credit report are rejected, it may be necessary to escalate your dispute using specific legal language to invoke the agency's legal obligations to remove mistakes from your record. This process can be time-consuming and may require specialized knowledge of the legal requirements for credit reporting to obtain success.

If you do find errors in your credit reports, the Fair Credit Reporting Act requires credit reporting agencies to correct these errors. But the agencies may not always respond promptly, or the first time you file a dispute. To be honest, they may try stall tactics, hoping that you give up so they don't have to spend the time and money to sort out what is correct and remove the erroneous information. It may be necessary to go through an escalation process to get errors removed or contact the creditor directly for help in proving your case.

When disputing a mistake on your credit report, compiling a list of supporting documents or witnesses is a good idea. If, for example, the status of one of your accounts is listed incorrectly or, God forbid, your name is spelled wrong, you will want to compile documents which show your proper account status or a birth certificate and Social Security card showing the proper spelling of your name.

You will want to send copies of the supporting documents—not the originals!—to the bureau whose report you are disputing. Keep the originals safe in case additional copies may be needed in the future.

If negative marks appear on your report, but these are *accurate*, you will want to turn your attention to settling your debts. In many cases, it is possible to move delinquent accounts into good standing within a few months through strategic spending and negotiations with your creditors.

Once your accounts are marked as current and in good standing, you can contact the credit bureau with the mistake to ask them to remove the negative marks from your obsolete account status.

If a credit reporting agency refuses to correct errors on your report or update it to reflect account status changes, there are services that can help you get erroneous or fraudulent marks removed from your credit reports successfully. My own business, Major League Credit & Lending, offers such a service. I sincerely hope you will never need to argue with a credit reporting agency about errors they refuse to remove from your report. But if you ever do, we can help.

If you have handled the dispute process to the fullest extent and appropriate changes still have not been made, you can file a complaint with the Consumer Financial Protection Bureau.[4] This is the primary organization in charge of ensuring that laws to protect consumers, including laws about accurate credit reporting, are followed.

If that still fails to produce results, as a last resort, you can file a lawsuit for violations of Fair Credit Reporting Act statutes. The National Association of Consumer Advocates may be able to help you find legal representation for such an endeavor.[56]

Let us all hope your credit reports remain error-free and are appropriately updated by credit reporting bureaus. But if this fails to happen for some reason, it's good to know that credit advisors, federal agencies, and advocacy organizations have your back and can enforce requirements and assist you in finding legal representation.

CHAPTER 6
BUILDING TIER 2 CREDIT

Now that you've taken some measures to begin to build your credit score, you will become eligible for more advanced trade accounts. It may take a few months, but once your business credit score begins to climb, you may secure better rewards, better interest rates, and higher credit limits on business tradeline accounts from major retailers.

What I call "Tier 2" credit refers to these more advanced tradelines, which may require some credit history to obtain, but which are largely similar to Tier 1 tradelines. Their higher limits and more complex and flexible terms will be good practice for the larger and more complex forms of financing we'll cover in Tiers 3 and 4.

Tier 2 credit tradelines should not require a personal guarantee to back up your line of credit, but they may offer the option of using one. In other words, they may ask whether you, as the business owner, would like to stake your personal credit score or some of your belongings on your promise to pay your invoices.

Giving a personal guarantee is not necessarily bad if you are 100% confident that you will buy no more from this creditor than you can afford to pay back. When using Tier 2 credit primarily to build business credit in order to work toward eventually obtaining bank loans and investors, the hope is that you would be planning to pay off 100% of your business purchases made on credit.

The idea here is not to accumulate too many hard inquiries early on or use credit to buy things you don't already have money for: the idea is to use credit to show that you can establish leverage and responsibly pay off loans so that you can be eligible for much more credit in the future.

So if you are completely sure that you will spend no more than you can easily pay back on a trade line, giving a personal guarantee may be fine. But if you feel any uncertainty about whether your business will be able to continue paying all its bills, or whether someone else in your business might use this tradeline irresponsibly, stick to credit tradelines that do not require a personal guarantee. You don't want to put your personal credit score or assets at risk if you feel any uncertainty about your business's ability to pay all its bills in the next year or so.

When applying for Tier 2 business credit, you will likely be asked for some or all of the following information to allow the vendors to research and verify your business:

- Documentation showing that your business is an entity in legal good standing with your Secretary of State.
- Your Employer Identification Number
- Your business address. This must match on all documents, so if you have more than one address, such as a mailing address and a physical address, choose one to use for your credit applications and stick with it!
- Your D-U-N-S number (this is why we had you apply for this a few months ago.)
- Proof of any licenses your business is required to have in your city and state.

- The information for your separate, dedicated business bank account.
- The phone number under which your business is listed in the 411 directory.

For this chapter, we will focus on vendors that have two attributes which are ideal for businesses seeking to build Tier 2 credit history rapidly. These three important attributes are:

1. Net 30 accounts. While some businesses prefer longer payment periods, Net 30 accounts are the fastest way to build credit history as they report your successful payments to credit bureaus just 30 days after they issue your invoice.
2. Reporting to at least two of the three major business credit reporting agencies. All the vendors we will recommend here report your successful payments to at least two of the following: Dun & Bradstreet, Equifax, and Experian.
3. All of these vendors allow you to pay their invoices with credit cards, including your Brex card. This allows you to have each of your successful payments reported to all three major credit bureaus, and even have your successful payments reported to some of them *twice*.

Any vendor that meets all three above requirements will allow you to rapidly build Tier 2 credit history and rapidly build toward being approved for a bank loan or obtaining investors or other high-caliber business financing options. I've assembled some examples of vendors we know to meet these requirements in this book.

EXAMPLES OF RECOMMENDED VENDORS

Amazon.com offers business tradeline accounts which allow businesses to take advantage of special wholesale pricing. These accounts do not require a personal guarantee from the business owner.

Amazon reports successful payments made to its business tradeline accounts to Dun & Bradstreet and to Equifax. This means that by making purchases through an Amazon business tradeline and paying your invoice using your Brex secured credit card, your business purchases are being reported to Equifax, Experian, and to Dun & Bradstreet *twice*. Talk about building business credit history!

Lowe's is another vendor that can be useful for businesses in certain industries. Lowe's reports to Equifax, Experian, and Dun & Bradstreet, meaning that if you pay your Lowe's invoice using a Brex credit card, your successful payment will be reported to Equifax once and to Experian and Dun & Bradstreet both twice. Now that's efficient.

Another example of a useful vendor is TigerDirect Electronics. Like Amazon business tradelines, business tradelines from TigerDirect offer special wholesale pricing on electronics that you may need for your business.

TigerDirect reports its payment history to Experian and Equifax, so when you pay your TigerDirect invoices with your Brex credit card, your payment history will be reported to Experian twice in addition to reporting to Equifax and D & B.

These are, of course, just examples of businesses offering Tier 2 business credit tradelines. Countless major retailers and suppliers offer credit tradelines to businesses that have some credit history.

To optimize your business's credit reports, choose vendors that report to at least two: Equifax, Experian, Dun & Bradstreet. Then pay your invoices to these vendors using your Brex credit card to stack your credit reporting history.[1]

Your business is now really building its credit history! With a few months' worth of payments to at least three Tier 1 vendors or credit-building resources under your belt, you're about to level up to adopt a Brex account and credit card and at least three Tier 2 vendors. We will now give all these accounts time to report to the bureaus, which can take up to 90 days.

I have never seen reporting take more than two months, but it's best not to plan anything absolutely requiring that credit reporting occur until 90 days have elapsed. This is another reason to closely monitor your business credit reports.

After these accounts are visibly reporting, it's time to build additional payment history by moving on to the next exciting step: applying for more advanced types of financing!

CHAPTER 7
TIER 3: REVOLVING & FLEET CREDIT CARDS

Now that you have credit history including Tier 1 and Tier 2 tradelines, we will move on to some truly advanced business credit.

Before applying for these Tier 3 business credit lines, you are going to want to have the following Tier 1 and Tier 2 tradelines to show a truly stellar credit history:

- 7 or more tradelines which report to Dun & Bradstreet. Remember, this can include your Tier 1 and Tier 2 tradelines. If you do not have at least six lines of business credit reporting to Dun & Bradstreet, you may wish to open more and allow one or two invoicing periods to pass before continuing to apply for Tier 3 credit.
- 3 or more tradelines which report to Experian.
- 3 or more tradelines which report to Equifax.
- At least one tradeline with a credit limit greater than $500.

I also recommend that you check your credit reports again if you have not already procured comprehensive credit-monitoring services. As with the last time you "leveled up," you want to know about any potential problems on your reports *before* you apply for these Tier 3 credit lines. Keep an eye out for any surprising or negative information and familiarize yourself with your business's current credit reports. Again, I highly recommend monitoring your business reports through Nav.com.

Once you're familiar with your reports and have taken action to correct any issues that may harm your business's image in the eyes of creditors, let's talk about Tier 3 credit.

In this chapter, we will discuss two kinds of Tier 3 credit.

- Tier 3 credit tradelines. These may offer big benefits to your business, but may not be as helpful to building your credit history as your Tier 1 and Tier 2 tradelines.

TIER 3 CREDIT TRADELINES

Tier 3 credit includes access to tradelines that are valuable for their own sake. Companies that may not offer credit accounts to new businesses without much credit history may offer significant benefits such as wholesale prices and rewards points to more established businesses that have thoroughly proven their ability to pay their invoices reliably.

These tradelines can offer massive value to your business if they improve your access to products your business may need. Some examples of major retailers who offer business credit tradelines to established businesses but not to businesses with little credit history include industry-specific hardware retailers such as flooring and auto parts suppliers, Sam's, Costco, United Airlines, Apple, Best Buy, and a large number of banks and credit unions that offer financial products including retirement portfolios and high-limit credit cards.

While these products may benefit your business, be aware that many of these Tier 3 credit vendors may NOT report your successful payments to them to credit reporting agencies. So take advantage of these elite credit lines if they benefit your business directly, but be aware that you may find that many of these do not help you directly build credit history on your credit report as they do not report to the credit bureaus.

These tier 3 credit vendors can, however, help with your credit history in two ways:

- If you pay your invoices using a business credit card that *does* report to major bureaus, such as your Brex card, you can still have your successful payments to these vendors reported through your credit card company's reporting.
- These credit lines can still act as "trade references." They will not show up on your public credit report if they don't report to the bureaus, so they will not help you qualify for loans or additional credit at first glance when your financier is accessing your public credit reports to decide whether to speak with you further. But if a bank or other financier decides you look promising enough to speak to, you may be given the opportunity to provide evidence of additional "trade references," at which point you can introduce these Tier 3 tradelines as additional evidence that your business is thriving and paying all its bills on time.

Moving up to Tier 3 credit offers some exciting possibilities as far as the types of tradelines you are eligible for and the purchasing power these can give your business. You are now well on your way to having access to tens of thousands of dollars in business financing, all with favorable terms like low-interest rates and long repayment periods!

CHAPTER 8
TIER 4: HIGH-LIMIT CASH LINES OF
CREDIT & MORE FLEET CREDIT

There are many echelons of business credit, from those occupied by the mega-corporations of the world to the Tier 1 credit used by new business owners who are just learning the ropes of business finance. In this book, we will move up through Tier 4, as this is the gateway into the level of financing at which rapid expansion into a franchise or large corporation can occur if you want it to.

Tier 4 credit includes a number of types of credit that are not typically available to new businesses and businesses without much-reported credit history. These include:

- Computer leases from major tech companies.
- Car financing from major car companies.
- Bank credit cards which may have very high credit limits, useful rewards programs, and other favorable terms.
- Financing from investors who may infuse large amounts of cash into your business and may also offer guidance in growing your business to the next level.

Even if you do not plan to seek investors, I recommend that you read this chapter to the end. This is because the questions investors ask can help businesses discover new ideas with the potential for massive business growth even without investors. After all, it is the investors' job to think about how companies can grow. Just like when making your business plan, considering how you would pitch your company to a venture capitalist if you absolutely *had* to get investors to keep your business going may force you to identify opportunities for growth via new inventions, product lines, or business models.

There are many ways you can explore the business credit lines offered by major tech companies, car companies, and other industry-specific vendors. For this chapter, we will focus on information that can be used by almost any business, such as advanced business credit cards and procuring investors.

Before applying for Tier 4 credit lines or pitching to investors, you will want to ensure that you have at least 14 business credit tradelines. These include your 7+ Tier 1 and Tier 2 credit-reporting lines, and any Tier 3 credit lines you may have opened, such as loans or non-reporting trade references.

While juggling 14 accounts may sound like a lot, remember that at this point, most of your business's operating supplies can likely be procured through business credit tradelines and that business credit cards you use to pay your vendor invoices also count as credit lines. If you split your monthly invoices between three or four business credit cards that all report to credit bureaus, for example, those will count as business tradelines on your credit reports without requiring you to buy more things or spend more money.

You are essentially paying for the same purchases twice, and having your purchases count as two separate payment experiences, by first buying from vendors and then paying your vendor invoices with a credit card which you then proceed to pay off in full each month.

If you don't yet have 14 business credit tradelines at this point, take some time to strategize how you might open more tradelines without increasing your cost or administrative burden too much. Is there a way you could use new tradelines to earn more rewards, or open a new business credit card that reports to multiple major credit bureaus and use that to pay some of your existing invoices?

Remember that this process of building credit is also a process of building your organizational and administrative skills. These are essential skills to making strategic decisions for a growing business, and they will serve you well if you choose to undertake massive business growth in the future!

I also recommend that you check your business credit reports before applying for Tier 4 credit or pitching to investors. It's always wise to make sure that there are no unforeseen developments you need to address before making a major financial move that requires your business to undergo the scrutiny of lenders and investors.

Because you are now entering a stage in your business development in which very large amounts of money, debt, and equity may be involved, I have one more warning before you proceed.

GET A LAWYER. NOW.

You must have any agreements with lenders or investors reviewed by a business attorney with whom you have a good relationship before you sign them.

I will say that again: this is *imperative*.

Many business owners go without a business lawyer in the earlier stages of their business to save money. Then, if they don't encounter problems as a result, they may be reluctant to begin paying a lawyer as they take on progressively more complex and high-stakes business agreements.

However, you must have an attorney look over any agreements with investors, and the more money you invest into borrowing through other forms of financing, the higher the stakes will be. This is the ownership and control over your business we are talking about here. It is not unheard of for unscrupulous investors and/or clueless business owners to create a situation where the investor has taken a large degree of ownership and control of a company without the business owner realizing it.

It is preferable to develop an ongoing relationship with a business lawyer whom you trust at this stage. If you are looking at potentially obtaining credit cards with $100,000 monthly credit limits, you have the necessary cash flow to warrant this.

Such lawyers may be helpful in looking over *all* contracts that your business uses or signs, since the more success your business has, the more money it may have to lose in the event of lawsuits or simply bad contracts which sign away too many rights.

So find a business lawyer that you trust *now* if you haven't already. It's time to make a good lawyer part of your business family.

TIER 4 BUSINESS CREDIT CARDS

Tier 4 business credit cards are designed for established businesses. This is why they aren't typically available to new businesses with extensive credit histories proving their ability to manage cash flow and pay their bills.

Once your business has sufficiently proven its financial prowess by building up credit history, you will become eligible for Tier 4 credit cards and other credit lines from companies such as:

- Frost Bank offers business credit cards with no annual fees and monthly credit limits of up to $100,000.
- American Express Corporate offers cards for businesses with less than $4 million in annual revenue which accrue rewards points that can be used with airlines and which, in some cases, may have *no* credit limit.
- Citizens Bank offers business credit cards with no annual fee and options to choose between low-interest rates and high reward points programs.

These are, of course, just a few examples of the top recommended business credit cards available to a business with Tier 4 credit. It is likely that nearly every bank and credit union offers some kind of elite business credit card. Some may require that your business have several million dollars in annual revenue in addition to a stellar credit score, but others may have options specifically for small business owners.

If these business credit cards sound interesting to you, now is the point where you may be well-qualified to apply for them. Take some time to research business credit card options offered by your local banks, or those which offer industry-specific discounts and rewards points that you may be able to use to cut your business's operating costs.

It's also time to consider whether you want to seek investors for your business. While investment capital can be a powerful tool for fueling massive business growth, keep in mind that investors may also ask for some control over company operations decisions, which may not be necessary for every business.

APPLY FOR A BREX BUSINESS ACCOUNT

Now that your business has some credit history from using the strategies discussed in our Tier 1 chapter, you may qualify for a Brex business account. A Brex account is similar to a bank account but is superior to a typical checking account in several ways.

Brex accounts are insured by the FDIC just like bank accounts are, but money held in Brex accounts can be sent via ACH or wired worldwide for free. Brex accounts also allow unlimited users and cards to be linked to your account, offer business rewards programs, and count toward your business credit history.

Brex can't replace your business bank account, but it can be an extremely useful tool if you want to build business credit history or make it easier to move money internationally, or make funds available to multiple members of your business.

Just remember that with great power comes great responsibility: if you are going to move money internationally or make it available to more members of your businesses, make sure to keep close tabs on that spending to ensure you will be able to pay all your invoices in full at the end of the month.

Once you have a Brex account, you will receive a Brex business card. This card is secured by the money you have in your Brex account, but it functions otherwise like a credit card. Brex reports your successful (or unsuccessful) payments on this credit card to Experian and Dun & Bradstreet.

I recommend that you use this card to make your invoice payments moving forward. In a way, this allows you to count your payment history toward your business credit history twice: once when you pay the vendors, and again when you pay Brex to cover those expenses.

Once you have built even more credit history by maintaining Tier 1-3 vendor accounts and paying off a secured Brex credit card for a few months, you will eventually qualify for an *unsecured* Brex credit card, which offers a higher limit and more rewards that your business can use. An unsecured Brex credit card represents tremendous purchasing power; by the time you get there, you will have cultivated the necessary skills to use it responsibly!

SEEKING INVESTORS

There are several tiers of investing, just as there are many tiers of business credit. When you investigate an established company's investors profile, you may find information saying that it has been through various "rounds" of financing. This can refer to investing from different types of investors who have specific business models for investing at companies in different stages of development.

As you will see from this section, getting investors can be quite a competitive and specialized endeavor. It can be even more challenging than getting a bank loan since investors are hoping that you will not merely manage to pay them back, but that your business will grow so much that the money they invest with you will be multiplied. I plan to release a whole book on the topic of how to get investors—and avoid signing bad investment agreements—in 2024.

For now, I wanted to include an overview of the process of getting investors here to demystify this process and give you an idea of what to expect and what to research further if your business decides to seek investors as a form of financing.

The first tier of investing for most businesses is called "angel investing." These are the investors who are most willing to invest in new businesses that have not previously worked with investors and who may be new to the business world altogether.

After you have finished reading this chapter, completed the recommended exercises, and compiled the recommended materials, you can begin to search for angel investors through the following organizations:

- Angel Capital Association
- Angel Investment Network
- Gust (formerly known as AngelSoft)

The second tier of investment for many businesses is called "venture capital funding." The name kind of says it all. Venture capitalists specialize in investing in new and relatively unproven businesses in hopes of "getting on the ground floor of the next big thing." The "venture" in "venture capital" refers to the fact that this is considered a little bit riskier and more uncertain than other types of investing, as we see below:

Venture:

Noun: A risky or daring journey or undertaking.

Verb: To dare to do something or go somewhere that may be dangerous or unpleasant.

—Oxford Languages

It is possible to obtain venture capital without first having obtained angel investors, although it can be more challenging.

Because angel investors and venture capital funds often seek similar things in the businesses they invest in, we will combine their requirements into a single section for the purposes of this book.

A venture capitalist's hope is that the company they invest in grows to become very large, and their investment's value will thus be multiplied. Imagine, for example, being one of the first investors in Apple. As a venture capitalist investing in Apple, you could have purchased a large number of Apple shares for a fraction of the current share price. You could have ended up owning a large chunk of the company for what would be a tiny investment compared to Apple's worth today.

Because venture capitalists choose businesses that are newer and less proven, they will want rigorous information about your company's past growth and plans for the future to convince them that you have the potential to grow by orders of magnitude in the years to come. Only then will they give you a large infusion of cash in exchange for partial ownership of your company.

Venture capital funds will also often serve as "fund managers," signaling to other investors that they believe in this company and inviting other investors to invest. They often charge an annual fee for managing the company's investment fund for a period of 7 to 10 years, during which they hope the company will establish rapid growth.

Because they will then have invested a great deal of their own money into your company's success, venture capitalists will also have an interest in providing guidance to optimize your company's chances of massive growth.

This may be very desired if you are a financially motivated business owner who wants your company to become as big as possible. On the other hand, it may be very undesired if you are a craft-driven business owner who wants to ensure that certain business practices or quality standards are adhered to, even if these may not be compatible with rapid growth into a large corporation.

This is why it's a good idea to carefully consider what your real goals are for your business. Some business owners are motivated by building as much personal and generational wealth as possible; others are motivated by something else entirely.

After a company is already fairly large and successful, investments from other types of entities become more likely. Many different types of investors exist who seek to invest in companies at different stages of their growth and in different situations. Larger businesses or business owners may seek to buy your company from you for a large amount of money, or to buy a stake in your company as a first step toward acquisition. Businesses whose cash flow and growth have stabilized may even "go public" and be traded on the stock market where the general public can invest by buying shares.

If you decide you want to seek investments and guidance from venture capitalists, how do you demonstrate to these investors that your business is an excellent prospect to invest in?

Venture capital companies look for companies with big potential for high ROI—return on investment—within a defined "investment horizon," or time limit, such as the 7-10 years mentioned above. This means that venture capitalists will be interested in many of the items you compiled for your business plan and financial projections when applying for a loan. They will want to know things like how you will use their money, what ROI you expect on that money, and how much you see your company's total cash flow and value growth over the next 7-10 years if you receive this funding.

Unlike most lenders, venture capitalists may also want the right and responsibility of seeking out opportunities for financial and business growth that you haven't spotted yet, such as new business practices, target audiences, marketing practices, or technologies. This is a valuable service for growth-minded business owners, but following these recommendations may also become a requirement after a venture capital fund has invested in your business.

The following is a list of things that angel investors and venture capitalists look for in their companies. Following these best practices may help optimize your business's chances of success and growth, even if you don't seek investors since these items are designed to assure venture capitalists that your business will grow wildly in the years to come.

#1: DISRUPTIVE POTENTIAL

Venture capitalists tend to particularly want to hear about your business's "disruptive" potential. In this case, "disruption" refers to your business having a business model, method, or technology that is so unique that it has the potential to "disrupt" the way business is currently done in your industry. This is why most venture capitalists are active in the tech space, where new technologies often fundamentally change the way we go about our everyday lives. But other new inventions, methods, or business models may also fit the bill for "disruptive" potential.

Companies with advantages when seeking venture capital include:

- Those that have invented a new technology which has capabilities other technologies don't have.
- Those whose products are markedly different from the competition or offer features not found in any other product.
- Disruptive business models, such as those that offer significant advantages over existing mainstream business models in operating costs or customer experience.

Some business owners who seek venture capital funding may feel that they do not have the potential to achieve it. If, for example, their business is not a tech business. Venture capital requirements can also spur business owners to think outside the box and discover ideas with potential for explosive growth. These attributes describe businesses that have the potential to rapidly outpace their competition through innovation and can create the potential for greater growth with or without venture capital funding.

#2 THE RIGHT TEAM

We've mentioned a few times throughout this book how important it is to have the right leadership team for business success. We've talked about how having business partners with less than sterling reputations can become a problem for your business's "family tree" in your Dun & Bradstreet report. Your business partners must be extremely trustworthy to be trusted with your business's money, and credit, and your team's expertise and experience are key to convincing lenders that your business will succeed and pay back the money they loan you with interest.

Venture capitalists take this to the next level. They know that the success of a business is more about the people running the business than about the business's ideas or technologies. Are the people in charge hard-working and dedicated to success? Do they have the emotional temperament to work together through the ups and downs of a new business and provide a positive experience for their business partners? Can they analyze their business's finances and make strategic business decisions to optimize growth?

Venture capital firms will want to see that your team has good ideas, technical expertise, emotional intelligence, and a track record of good decision-making. This doesn't mean you all have to be perfectly prim and proper; often, people with a bit of a risk-taking streak do best in business. But you will want a team that demonstrates a commitment to the success of your business, an ability and willingness to make strategic decisions and change course as needed, and the emotional resilience to handle conflicts and crises that might arise during the course of a young business's life.

Venture capitalists will look for these things—but they are also things that any business can benefit from.

Now is a good time to analyze your leadership team honestly

and look for any weak points in these areas. Are there points that could be improved upon? Is there some kind of training or coaching you or your business partners could procure to make you better executives who are best suited to take the actions necessary to grow your business?

#3 THE RIGHT MARKET

One major indicator of a business's likely future success is the general market demand for its product. If you are in a business selling products that have been rendered obsolete by a new invention, for example, you had better innovate your product offerings fast! On the other hand, if you are selling a product or service that is rapidly growing in popularity, you are likely to experience growth even if you are not one of the most stream-lined players in that industry.

As such, venture capitalists will want to see numbers regarding your overall target market. "Target market" encompasses both your industry—the market for the specific type of good or service you provide—and demand for your good or service within a specific target demographic if you have one.

If, for example, you are particularly good at solving a problem that affects mostly people of a certain socioeconomic background, educational background, or cultural background, that could give you an advantage or disadvantage depending on whom your product or service is specialized for.

Can you find numbers to indicate whether demand for your product or service is currently rising or falling? Are there specific groups of people among whom the demand is rising? If demand for your product or service is falling, is there a way you can pivot to provide products and services that meet the changing demands of the market?

Venture capitalists will want to see the most specific numbers possible regarding the demand for your product in today's market. And you will want to see these numbers as a business owner, as they will help you plan for the years ahead.

#4 SALES

Generally, venture capitalists will want to see that you already have a track record of steadily growing sales over the lifespan of your company. The more sales growth you're able to demonstrate, the more likely venture capitalists are to believe that more growth is very likely in your future.

Have you been able to demonstrate growth in sales? If not, how can you prioritize that right now? What are the missing parts of your sales or marketing process that are preventing sales growth?

Even if you are not seeking to procure venture capitalist funding, buckling down and learning how to grow sales is an important growth step for you as a business owner.

#5 FINANCIAL PLAN

This financial plan has many things in common with the business plan we discussed when applying for business loans. Venture capitalists will want to see how you plan to allocate your current funds and your investment funds to areas like:

- Advertising
- Expansion
- Acquisition of new resources
- Outsourcing non-core functions to optimize your results and your revenue.

Seeing how exactly you plan to allocate funds to these areas gives venture capitalists a good idea of your likelihood of success. Putting together such a plan, including using any current numbers available for costs, revenue, and ROI for each component of your business's operations, can help you grow your business massively with or without investment funding.

#6 FUTURE PROJECTIONS

Venture capital funds will want to see detailed breakdowns of your costs and profits from your business's years to date and detailed projections of what you can reasonably expect your finances to look like in future years.[1]

Use the specifics you put together for your financial plan to project in detail exactly how much growth you can reasonably expect to see based on your costs, revenue, and ROI details in combination with your plans for spending investment capital.

The result should be a solid plan for turning investment capital—or any other kind of capital you receive, such as loans, credit lines, and your own growing revenue—into larger and larger profits each year.

You may or may not choose to pursue investors for your business. But either way, you can learn a lot about streamlining your business for growth and how innovation can help you to grow by answering the questions investors ask when considering whether to invest in a business.

I hope that this chapter leaves you with renewed insight into how your brand can innovate, change, and grow with changing times, as well as increased purchasing power!

CHAPTER 9
BUSINESS LOANS

We've now seen how building business credit can create some truly impressive financing options. But what about that often-discussed holy grail of small business owners, the business loan?

KNOW YOUR LOAN OPTIONS

So far in this book, we have focused on what credit bureaus call "revolving tradelines." These are tradelines whose value turns over, or "revolves" on a regular basis. Credit lines where you make purchases on credit and then pay off those purchases on a regular basis are revolving tradelines.

Loans and mortgages, on the other hand, are "installment tradelines." This refers to the fact that, instead of borrowing money and paying it back in a revolving fashion, you borrow one large amount of money and then pay it back in installments over the course of months or years.

Successfully paying off a loan for years to come requires a certain level of financial stability, foresight, and planning, which is why installment tradelines like loans and mortgages are typically difficult to get approved for unless you already have spectacular credit history and cash flow. This is also why most new business owners who apply for a loan while their business is still in its infancy are denied: lenders simply don't have the confidence that they have the skill and cash flow necessary to pay off a loan that may total tens or hundreds of thousands of dollars.

The good news is you now have the skills and the credit history of making this happen. If you have successfully been paying off seven or more Tier 1 and Tier 2 tradelines for four to six months, you have both demonstrated reliability and developed the planning and cash management skills necessary to add installment payments on a loan to your business' list of monthly bills.

If you want a large infusion of cash in the form of a business loan, you now have sufficient credit history that lack of credit history is not likely to be an obstacle when you apply.

However, as you will see in this section, many types of loans exist, and different types may be right for different businesses. In addition, applying for loans is a very competitive process, and there is a science to impressing different kinds of lenders. Having a stellar business credit report is almost always essential to obtain a good loan, but other aspects of your loan application will also be important. I plan to release an entire book to cover this subject in more depth later in 2023, so stay tuned for details.

For now, I wanted to include an overview of the process of applying for loans to give you an idea of the basic types available and the basic steps involved. If you feel that applying for a loan for you is right now, you can seek out my book or other resources to learn more details about what to look for in a great loan for your business model and how exactly to wow a loan officer.

Many types of small business loans exist. When comparing the options available to you, consider questions like:

- Why do you need the funding? How will you use it to increase your profit to the point that it's easy to pay back the loan while building massive wealth on top of the repayment cost?

- How fast do you need the money? Some types of loans take longer to approve than others, and larger loans are often slower to be approved.
- How much money do you really need? Will you benefit more from a $500,000 investment, or will $50,000 get the job done and allow your business to level up?
- What will be the total cost of debt if you take this loan? Consider factors like interest rates and any penalties for early repayment (some banks will charge fees if you repay your loan early because the interest that accrues over time is their source of profit). A good accountant or financial advisor may be helpful to you when analyzing these questions.

Several types of business loans are available that you may wish to investigate. These include:

- Bank loans. These can range in size from $10,000 to $1,000,000. They can be more challenging to get than some types of loans, but they also tend to have lower interest rates than loans that are easier to obtain, so if you get approved you will likely save money over time.
- Small Business Administration loans. The Small Business Administration is an agency run by the federal government with the mission of helping small businesses to grow and thrive. The approval process for SBA loans can be slow, but they offer a wide range of interest rates from low to high and can offer longer repayment terms than other loan types meaning you will have longer to pay back the money. They can range in size from $30,000 to $5,000,000.
- Business term loans. These may be offered by online lenders, and range in size from $100 to $500,000. They typically have shorter repayment terms, which is good

if you want to get debt off your plate quickly, but not so great if you'd rather have a longer time to repay. They can also have higher interest rates than other loan types, so read the terms carefully. They may be best to use for one-time purchases such as equipment. However, there is also…

- Equipment financing. This is a form of financing specifically for buying equipment for your business. It is a bit like a lease in that the lender agrees to pay for some or all of the cost of your equipment and its installation, and you repay them gradually over time. However, if you cannot make your payments, the lender can repossess your equipment. These loans can have lower interest rates than business-term loans, but are obviously less flexible in how they can be used.

Which type of funding sounds best to you?

Would you rather go through a slow approval process for the chance at lower interest rates, or do you want to be assured of having money soon? Do you want to borrow a large amount to purchase a property or buy a large expansion for your equipment or staff, or would you rather have a smaller loan to pay for modest growth? Would you like to have many years to pay off a big loan, or would you like to get the debt off your plate quickly with a term loan? Would equipment financing help you to grow while minimizing the amount you need to repay?

Once you have decided what types of business loans look best to you, the next step is applying. This is a time to be strategic, because applying for a business loan may constitute a "hard inquiry" which can temporarily take points off your credit score. Therefore, it's a good idea to identify the two or three loans that seem best to you. I recommend starting by applying to your favorite first when your credit score is best, and sending out subsequent applications one at a time if your first application does not succeed.

It is also good to seek lenders like those recommended by my company, Major League Credit & Lending, who offer pre-approvals first and will not cost a hard inquiry until you accept the loan agreement. You can avoid many hard inquiries by getting pre-approved for financing. In some cases, having your bank's pre-approval for financing may even allow you to obtain other types of credit lines without them feeling the need to send a hard inquiry since they already have your bank's promise to finance you and most likely a recent credit report.

When you have zeroed in on your favorite loan options, you will probably find information about what your business needs to qualify for these loans successfully. Look for information like:

- What business credit scores are preferred or required.
- Whether the lender prefers or requires that your business has operated for a certain period of time. Some will require several years of successful business history before making a large loan.
- Does the lender prefer or require a certain amount of cash flow from a business? Some may prefer to only give large loans to businesses who already have seven-figure annual cash flows.
- Does the loan require collateral, such as a personal guarantee or security through assets? If so, decide how comfortable you are with this. Are you confident enough that the funding will allow you to build wealth, or would you prefer to keep your personal credit score and assets protected?

Now that you've researched your options, it's a good idea to make sure your business plan is in ship shape.

Have you learned what is most profitable for your business model and warrants changes to your business plan? Have there been changes to items such as your leadership team, your marketing plan, or your financials since you first wrote your business plan?

This is a good time to revisit the section on business plans toward the end of Chapter 2. If you have been following our six-month plan, you may have learned a lot about what does and doesn't work to make your business profitable by now. You may also have expanded your cash flow using the credit lines you've acquired over the last four months. Your newly gained experience and knowledge will help you make the most impressive possible business plan to show to lenders.

Use this as an opportunity to optimize your business finances and operations as well. You may realize something while updating your business plan that could help you to make more money if implemented across your company.

Once your business plan is up-to-date and looks great, you will also want to create a funding request for your potential lenders. Explain how much funding you are asking for and why. Do you want debt or equity, and why have you made that choice? What repayment term would you like, and why? What will you do with the loan money?

If possible, use your funding request to break down a budget for how you will spend the loan money and cite any numbers that lead you to believe you will get a positive return on investment.

Consider questions like how much revenue an average employee, store location, or piece of equipment generates for you if you plan to use loan money to pay for these. Consider questions like what kind of ROI your history and research suggests you can get from the marketing campaign you have planned if you plan to use the funding to do marketing. The more specific numbers and details you can cite to convince lenders that you will make a positive return on investment for the loan money you spend, the more likely they will be to grant your loan.

You may also wish to include financial projections in your business plan and/or funding request. Include income statements, balance sheets, and cash flow statements from your business's past five years (if your business has been around that long). Include projections for how you expect these numbers to change over time if you are able to secure loan money and subsequently pay for additional employees, locations, equipment, marketing, etc.

You can download some examples from the Small Business Administration's website, or by visiting the link in this footnote.[1]

Your business plan is an excellent place to consolidate information for your potential lender, and it will also help you gain insight into the possible ways your business can grow. Once you have assembled your business plan, you will also want to gather...

YOUR LONG-TERM BUSINESS GOALS

In addition to your business plan, your potential lender will want to hear about your long-term business goals. This is important because there are several strategies business owners use when seeking to make a living or a profit off of a business.

Some business owners start their business because they just love providing that product or service. Such a business owner may wish to remain in control of their company until they retire. This will affect whether they want to seek investors who may bring financing and expertise to the business, but who may also desire some control over business decisions and decisions about daily operations. Such a business owner may want to plan to sell the company to another business owner at a large profit when they retire or may wish to pass on leadership to a trusted friend or family member, which means training a family member or other protégé instead of preparing the company to be sold.

Other business owners may be very financially minded. They may seek to profit financially as much as possible, as quickly as possible. This can mean putting the business on a fast track to attract investors or being sold to another company for a large sum. Existing companies will often buy highly profitable small businesses from their owners for large sums since they are essentially purchasing the company's profits for years to come. Some entrepreneurs even make a business model out of repeatedly starting companies and then selling them to larger companies when they have become highly successful.

Insomnia Cookies is an example of a company which was founded less than twenty years ago as a cookie delivery service based out of a student's dorm room and is now a huge national chain that its founders sold to Krispy Kreme. We don't know how much Krispy Kreme paid for the controlling stake in Insomnia Cookies, but it's a safe bet that it was at least in the millions.

None of these types of success happen without strategic planning. This is why it is essential to know your long-term goal. When you retire, do you want to sell your company for millions of dollars? Do you want that to be ten years from now or fifty years from now? Is it more important to you to keep the company in the family as a form of generational wealth, or to make sure that it's run in the right way, such that you may wish to retain ownership or pass ownership to a trusted individual? If you are more focused on making money than controlling your company's operations, do you want to attract investors?

What are the best practices followed by business owners who have found success in achieving their personal long-term goals for their business?

Being able to articulate your long-term vision for your company and why you have chosen that vision will tell your potential lenders that you are thinking strategically and will make strategic financial decisions—including the necessary decisions to pay them back!

TIME TO APPLY

When applying for your dream loan, be sure to read the requirements to determine what documents you will need.

Having your business plan and long-term business goal in mind is always a good idea, but different lenders may also require you to bring tax returns, cash flow sheets, business licenses, proof of patents or copyrights, and other legal documents to verify the information on your business plan and to prove that you are in good legal standing with all relevant government authorities.[2]

Read the requirements of each individual loan and lender and be sure to also take note of such specific details as their expected turnaround time. Some types of loans may grant approval within days or even minutes, while others may take weeks or months to get back to you. Don't assume that a faster turnaround time is better; those who take longer may do so because they are evaluating many competing businesses which all want their favorable loan terms.

WHAT DO YOU CHOOSE?

Now that you have an established business credit history, you can make big decisions about your company's future. Do you want to expand and build wealth as quickly as possible, or dedicate your attention to your craft and community? Do you want a big business loan to enable rapid expansion, or do you want to keep your installment payments low? Do you want to sell your company for millions of dollars someday, or keep it all in the family?

The sky is the limit when you make strategic business decisions. The truth is, everyone can run a business that is capable of massive growth; it is just a matter of asking the right questions and making strategic decisions.

As you can see from this chapter so far, applying for business loans can be quite a complex undertaking, so I'm working on an upcoming book about the subject which will cover topics like different types of loans available to you, red flags, and green flags to look for before signing a loan agreement, and optimizing your application to make the most robust possible case to your lender for why your business is an excellent candidate to receive this loan. I hope this book will assist those of you who want to move on to this next step of applying for business financing in the form of loans.

CHAPTER 10
GO FORTH AND GROW!

I am honored that you have chosen me to assist you on your business credit journey. This work means so much to me, as it means helping individuals to build personal and generational wealth.

You have now completed a comprehensive crash course on going from not having a business at all to procuring elite business credit lines, business loans, and potentially even investors who can guide you to massive business growth. I hope you can execute as many of these steps as you wish to make your business goals a reality.

Remember that building business credit and procuring financing takes time and perseverance. There is a tried and tested system which has a very high success rate for allowing any business owner to procure large amounts of financing for their business—but procuring success requires following these steps meticulously and in order.

I expect the completion of these steps to take between four months to a year for most business owners. In that time, you will grow tremendously as a business owner and a person.

In filing the necessary paperwork, you will gain fortitude, and the legal protections afforded by incorporating your business and separating its finance and liabilities from your own.

In procuring Tier 1 and Tier 2 business credit, you will grow your organizational and money management skills, and establish your business's credibility as a solid and legitimate corporation as a matter of public record.

In procuring Tier 3 and 4 business credit, you will gain access to vast amounts of business funding and financing—likely more than you now believe is possible. You will also ask advanced questions and assemble advanced cost-benefit analyses and financial projections, which will arm you with the knowledge and mindset you need to create genuinely massive growth for your business if you choose to do so.

If you want your business to remain small and craft-focused, that's okay. But if you want to become a national corporation with multiple locations, that is also within your reach if you follow the best practices listed here and continue to research further into some of the areas we have only briefly addressed.

Everything is within your reach. It's just a matter of combining strategic knowledge of business and finance with hard work and dedication.

That's the lesson I've learned on my own journey from never-run-a-business entrepreneur to founder and owner of multiple businesses. That's the lesson I wanted to share in this book, and it is a lesson that I hope will empower you and your loved ones with the necessary knowledge to take control of your lives.

If you have a moment, it would be very helpful to me and others if you could review this book on Amazon and/or Audible. Your review will help direct others to this book who may benefit from the knowledge it contains.

I wish you the best of luck and am so excited about your journey!

Leave a 1-Click Review!

I would be incredibly thankful if you could take just 60 seconds to write a brief review on Amazon, even if it's just a few sentences!

>> Click here to leave a quick review

AFTERWORD

Thank you for taking the time to make it to the end. In conclusion, we've learned a lot about the values of entrepreneurship, business and personal credit, and how you can use them to propel yourself forward no matter your resources or circumstances.

The wealth gap in America has severely separated the poor from the wealthy, not because people lack the ability, but because many lack the information and guidance to measure up. However, following many of the same tactics mentioned in this book, I have been able to overcome hurdles and leverage my creditworthiness, lendability, and knowledge to grow my business and brand - these methods work!

If you are unsure or a bit nervous about the process, again, my company Major League Credit & Lending has a complete business credit-building system that will walk you through each step from A-Z of starting your business and obtaining the startup capital that you need. You can do this without current cash flow, jeopardizing your personal credit, or having collateral. In fact, you are guaranteed to acquire at least $50,000 in funding in the first 6-12 months if you follow the blueprint.

Feel free to explore more information about all the business services I offer on my website at https://majorleaguecr.com/ or schedule a free consultation here https://majorleaguecr.com/business-credit-consultation. On the website, you will learn more about the platform, other business funding options, personal loans, and even consumer financing for your clients or customers.

Peace and blessings,

Chevon

OTHER BOOKS YOU'LL LOVE!

The Credit Game: Plays We Were Never Taught

Retirement Planning Handbook

FREE GIFT FOR READERS

JUST FOR YOU!

Or Visit: https://www.bit.ly/TCGgift

RESOURCES

NAV Business Credit Monitoring https://nav.nkwcmr.net/oejqZ9

FREE Consultation - calendly.com/majorleaguecreditrepair

Personal Credit Dispute Kit

https://drive.google.com/drive/folders/1uOHmqTXWl-ca42CtMusYeeI1omvizPihy?usp=sharing

Opus Virtual Office https://www.opusvirtualoffices.com/aff2/majorleaguecreditrepair/

Regus Virtual Office https://www.myregus.com/

Experian http://www.experian.com

Small Business Administration http://www.sba.gov

Dun & Bradstreet http://www.dnb.com/

Equifax http://www.equifax.com

Free Gift https://bit.ly/TCGgift

Leave a Review https://www.amazon.com/review/create-review/edit?ie=UTF8&channel=glance-detail&asin=B0BDSRQL4M

*may earn commissions

NOTES

INTRODUCTION

1. *5 surprising ways your business is impacted by poor credit: FleetCardsUSA*. Fleet-CardUSA. (n.d.). Retrieved October 7, 2022, from https://fleetcardsusa.com/blog/five-surprising-ways-your-business-is-impacted-by-poor-credit/
2. *10 stats that explain why business credit is important for small business*. U.S. Small Business Administration. (n.d.). Retrieved October 7, 2022, from https://www.sba.gov/blog/10-stats-explain-why-business-credit-important-small-business

1. YOUR BUSINESS CREDIT STRATEGY

1. Anna.Baluch. (2019, October 17). *What is tier 1 credit?* Experian. Retrieved November 4, 2022, from https://www.experian.com/blogs/ask-experian/what-is-tier-1-credit/

2. BUILD YOUR FOUNDATION

1. How to name a business in 5 simple steps (2022). The BigCommerce Blog. (2022, August 24). Retrieved October 7, 2022, from https://www.bigcommerce.com/blog/how-to-name-a-business/
2. Staff, D. (2022, June 28). *Is domain squatting still a factor in 2022? here's the lowdown*. Digital.com. Retrieved October 7, 2022, from https://digital.com/best-domain-registrars/domain-squatting/
3. Drake Forester - June 27, 2019. (2022, May 6). Should you incorporate your business in another state? SCORE. Retrieved October 7, 2022, from https://www.score.org/blog/should-you-incorporate-your-business-another-state
4. *Apply for an employer identification number (EIN) online*. Internal Revenue Service. (n.d.). Retrieved October 8, 2022, from https://www.irs.gov/businesses/small-businesses-self-employed/apply-for-an-employer-identification-number-ein-online
5. McCraw, C., & Guzman, M. D. (2022, March 10). *Google Voice Review: Is it right for your business?* Fit Small Business. Retrieved October 8, 2022, from https://fitsmallbusiness.com/google-voice-review/

3. ESTABLISH (AND FIX!) YOUR BUSINESS CREDIT REPORTS

1. Rashkovich, B. (2020, August 11). *FICO SBSS business credit score: How to understand and improve yours.* Fundera. Retrieved October 20, 2022, from https://www.fundera.com/blog/fico-sbss#sources
2. Rashkovich, B. (2020, August 11). *FICO SBSS business credit score: How to understand and improve yours.* Fundera. Retrieved October 20, 2022, from https://www.fundera.com/blog/fico-sbss#sources

4. BUSINESS CREDIT TIER 1: NET 30 ACCOUNTS

1. "NET Terms Guide: What Are NET 30/60/90 Terms?" Resolve. Accessed December 13, 2022. https://resolvepay.com/blog/post/net-terms/.
2. "Online Home Store for Furniture, Decor, Outdoors & More." Wayfair. Accessed December 13, 2022. https://www.wayfair.com/.
3. "Office Supplies, Cleaning Supplies & More for Every Workspace." Cleaning & Office Supplies for Every Workspace | Quill.com. Accessed December 13, 2022. https://www.quill.com/.
4. "Compare Credit Options - Office Depot." officedepot.com. Accessed December 13, 2022. https://www.officedepot.com/l/credit/compare?cm_sp=marketing-_-FooterAds-Credit-_-Footer-Ads-Ad2-Footer%3Fcm_sp.
5. *Shipping boxes, shipping supplies, packaging materials, packing supplies.* ULINE. (n.d.). Retrieved December 13, 2022, from https://www.uline.com/
6. *Grainger Industrial Supply - MRO products, equipment and Tools.* Grainger Industrial Supply - MRO Products, Equipment and Tools. (n.d.). Retrieved December 13, 2022, from https://www.grainger.com/
7. ECREDABLE pricing. eCredable Small Business. (n.d.). Retrieved December 13, 2022, from https://business.ecredable.com/Pricing
8. *Creditstrong business - get a business credit builder loan.* Credit Strong. (2022, July 15). Retrieved December 13, 2022, from https://www.creditstrong.com/business/

5. MONITOR BUSINESS CREDIT REPORTS

1. *Consumer Portal.* LexisNexis. (n.d.). Retrieved December 13, 2022, from https://consumer.risk.lexisnexis.com/request
2. *Request ChexSystems consumer disclosure report.* ChexSystems. (n.d.). Retrieved December 13, 2022, from https://www.chexsystems.com/request-reports/consumer-disclosure
3. Davies, A. (2020, April 28). *What is credit monitoring and is it effective?* American Express Credit Cards, Rewards & Banking. Retrieved November 4, 2022, from https://www.americanexpress.com/en-us/credit-cards/credit-intel/credit-monitoring/
4. *Submit a complaint.* Consumer Financial Protection Bureau. (n.d.). Retrieved December 13, 2022, from https://www.consumerfinance.gov/complaint/

5. *National Association of Consumer Advocates.* NACA. (n.d.). Retrieved December 13, 2022, from https://www.consumeradvocates.org/
6. Wells, L. (n.d.). *How to clear up your ChexSystems record.* Bankrate. Retrieved December 13, 2022, from https://www.bankrate.com/banking/how-to-clear-up-chexsystems-report/#second-chance-account

6. BUILDING TIER 2 CREDIT

1. Square Biz. (2022, March 17). *The best way to get tier 2 net 30 accounts.* YouTube. Retrieved December 14, 2022, from https://www.youtube.com/watch?v=cojsQ0W8lpE

8. TIER 4: HIGH-LIMIT CASH LINES OF

1. Admin. (2022, February 17). *VC funding: 7 rules to secure funding for startups.* 7 startup. Retrieved December 14, 2022, from https://www.7startup.vc/post/vc-funding-7-rules-to-secure-funding-for-startups/

9. BUSINESS LOANS

1. *Write your business plan.* Small Business Administration. (n.d.). Retrieved December 14, 2022, from https://www.sba.gov/business-guide/plan-your-business/write-your-business-plan
2. Furgison, L. (2020, March 3). *How to secure a business loan: Tips from a banking executive.* Bplans Blog. Retrieved December 14, 2022, from https://articles.bplans.com/how-to-secure-a-business-loan-tips-from-a-banking-executive/

Made in the USA
Columbia, SC
05 October 2024

43721027R00074